INTRODUCTION TO E
Series editor: Jonatha

370. 19345

GENDER AND SCHOOLS

GENDER AND SCHOOLS

Lynda Measor and Pat Sikes

CASSELL

Cassell
Villiers House
41/47 Strand
London WC2N 5JE

387 Park Avenue South
New York, NY 10016-8810

British Library Cataloguing-in-Publication Data
A catalogue record for this book is available from the
British Library.

ISBN 0-304-32401-9 (hardback)
      0-304-32397-7 (paperback)

Typeset by Colset Private Limited, Singapore
Printed and bound in Great Britain by Biddles Ltd,
Guildford and Kings Lynn

CONTENTS

This book is dedicated to our daughters, Lexie and Robyn.

ACKNOWLEDGEMENTS

We have very much appreciated the comments and advice received from Barry Troyna. Special thanks also go to our families, who have put up with us while we have been writing this book.

FOREWORD

The 1980s and 1990s have witnessed unprecedented changes to the education system. These have had a dramatic impact, particularly in relation to:

- schools' relationships with parents and the community;
- the funding and management of schools;
- the curriculum;
- the assessment of children's learning.

It can be an extremely daunting task for student teachers to unravel the details and implications of these initiatives. This Introduction to Education series therefore offers a comprehensive analysis and evaluation of educational theory and practice in the light of recent developments.

The series examines topics and issues of concern to those entering the teaching profession. Major themes representing a spectrum of educational opinion are presented in a clear, balanced and analytic manner.

The authors in the series are authorities in their field. They emphasize the need to have a well-informed and critical teaching profession and present a positive and optimistic view of the teacher's role. They endorse the view that teachers have a significant influence over the extent to which any legislation or ideology is translated into effective classroom practice.

Each author addresses similar issues, which can be summarized as:

- presenting and debating theoretical perspectives within appropriate social, political, and educational contexts
- identifying key arguments

- identifying individuals who have made significant contributions to the field under review
- discussing and evaluating key legislation
- critically evaluating research and highlighting implications for classroom practice
- providing an overview of the current state of debate within each field
- describing the features of good practice

The books are written primarily for student teachers. However, they will be of interest and value to all those involved in education.

Jonathan Solity
Series Editor

CHAPTER 1

Introduction

The chief distinction in the intellectual powers of the two sexes is shown by man attaining to a higher eminence in whatever he takes up, than woman can attain – whether requiring deep thought, reason, or imagination, or merely the use of the senses and hands.

(Charles Darwin, *The Descent of Man*, 1871)

This was written over one hundred years ago and it is unlikely that anyone now would make so strong a case for the inferiority of women. However, we want to argue that there is still a belief that women and men are noticeably different in their intellectual capacities and perhaps in the way they think. The more general problem of women's inequality has not disappeared in British society. There is systematic inequality between men and women in, for example, the labour market, education, social welfare and politics.

Feminists, angered by the injustice of this situation, began to investigate the scale of the problem and its causes and consequences. They drew attention to the part played in women's inequality by the education system.

The theme of this book is the significance of gender in education and what feminist research over the last two decades has discovered about it. The first issue is gender socialization: how do pupils learn to be boys or girls and what part do schools play in that process? Children have developed clear views about the right ways for girls and boys to behave before they come to school. The suggestion is that in school these ideas are reinforced and fixed in a number of different ways.

The second issue concerns the implications gender has for achievement in school. The feminist argument is that gender differentiation processes result in different educational experiences for women and men, which seem to give rise to contrasting educational achievements between the sexes and in the end to prepare each sex to occupy quite different roles and styles in life. Feminists argue that these experiences also result in girls 'underachieving', and that schools make a significant contribution to the inequality that exists between the sexes in society.

INEQUALITY AND EDUCATION

There is concern that education systems do not operate fairly for all pupils, that pupils' chances of doing well in school do not depend only on their 'ability' but vary according to their sex, social class and 'race'.

Sociologists recognize that schools are a sophisticated mechanism for selection, allocating pupils to a particular 'track' or stream that is deemed to be appropriate to their future position in the labour force. Conservative thinkers argue that schools select pupils on the basis of their talents and thus ensure that the best and brightest students will get the most senior and responsible positions in society. Most sociologists are unhappy with this cheerful view: they feel that schools do operate in unfair ways and tend to disadvantage and even discriminate against certain kinds of student. They emphasize that it is not necessarily the best pupils who reach the top of the heap.

For many years the main concern of researchers was male pupils from a working-class background, who were seen to be disadvantaged in and by schools. More recently gender has been receiving attention. It is recognized that girls and more specifically working-class girls are one of the groups who leave school unqualified or inadequately qualified. Black pupils are another group who significantly underachieve in British schools.

It is important to try to define what we mean by 'underachievement'. One aspect is certainly qualifications, which are the end point of schooling, and therefore important. It is clear that some children leave school unable to compete for high-status and well-paying jobs in the open labour market, because they lack appropriate qualifications. In this sense they underachieve, and Britain is left with workforce and skill shortages which hamper economic performance.

Although this is a controversial view, it seems to us that schools are or should be about more than just qualifications. Some writers have seen education as important for citizenship and crucial for maintaining a democratic nation. Humanist thinkers have seen education as having a unique function in liberating the individual and enabling us to achieve our full potential. This discussion opens up important questions about what we think are the purposes of schools. There are no simple answers to these questions and it is inevitably very difficult to assess the way in which children 'underachieve', in the sense that their ability to live full lives is not realized.

Schools are not solely responsible for this underachievement; girls receive a number of messages from home and community and from the mass media which work to 'turn them off' schooling. Nevertheless schools do play a part. Research makes it clear that despite the passing of sex discrimination legislation in 1975, and notwithstanding the many changes that have occurred, girls and women in education are still seriously disadvantaged and discriminated against in relation to boys and men. This is not to say that men may not be disadvantaged too, especially if they are of working-class origin or black. In this book, however, we concentrate on what happens to girls, because it is girls who still are the most disadvantaged in schools in comparison with boys, and women who are disadvantaged in the wider society in comparison with men.

It is of course the case that national government and local authorities have in recent years undertaken equal opportunities work in the education system. They have attacked the inequalities of class, and it is possible to argue that the 1944 Education Act was a significant example of this. Education is a political issue and governments have different priorities. Promoting equality in and through education has not been equally important to all governments since 1944.

In recent years gender and 'race' have been put on to the agenda as well. It is not difficult to argue that governments and local authorities need to do more to promote equal opportunities for all children: the issue is primarily one of social justice. The argument is that discrimination on grounds of race, sex, etc. is contrary to natural justice and is therefore morally unacceptable. Social justice is not the only issue, however. For most educationalists the full development of individual potential in every child is an important principle: 'Equal opportunity work puts the emphasis on the fostering of individual talent and potential and aims to remove any barriers to this full development' (Carr, 1989, p. 18).

The educational justification for tackling sexism and gender issues generally is that by doing so the quality of educational provision overall is improved. Carr suggests that when teachers and others involved with education work on gender issues it results in a clarification of objectives, the formulation of consciously worked out policies and an emphasis on effective evaluation, all of which improve the standards of teaching.

THE STRUCTURE OF THE BOOK

Since the 1970s there has been substantial interest in the issue of gender and education. In this book we aim to provide an overview of the material which has been written on the subject in that time. It is, however, the case that new works are constantly appearing and we provide some suggestions about useful sources of new material in this field in Appendix 1.

In Chapters 1–3 we introduce the controversial questions about the causes of gender differences and their consequences for schooling. We review the feminist arguments that have developed and look at the ways they account for women's inequality in society. We also consider the background to the issue, reviewing the history of the provision of different education for boys and girls. Lastly we provide an account of the legislation in Britain that is relevant to the issue of gender inequality in our schools.

In Chapters 4–7 we look at the experience of nursery, primary and secondary schooling and ask what schools are like for girls and boys. We analyse the factors of school organization, the curriculum and hidden curriculum and teachers' styles and attitudes. We also take account of the experience of adolescence and the effect that adolescent youth cultures have on pupils' attitudes to school. We then look at the relative career chances of male and female teachers in primary and secondary schools in Britain.

In the last chapter our intention is to document recent innovations and programmes which have attempted to promote equal opportunities in terms of gender in British schools. In conclusion we aim to provide a critical assessment of these programmes, and ask to what extent they have met their objectives.

THE SIGNIFICANCE OF GENDER

In this introductory chapter we look at the controversial questions about the causes of gender differences. We first introduce the key concepts, like sex and gender and sex role learning. We then go on to look at the debate about whether gender characteristics are natural or produced by society. Lastly we look at the different theories of gender socialization.

MEN AND WOMEN: THE DIFFERENCES BETWEEN THE SEXES

What do we mean when we classify people as male or female, men or women? On what characteristics and differences do we base the classification? The starting point for feminist thinkers is often the distinction between sex and gender (Oakley, 1972).

Sex

Sex refers to the most basic physiological differences between men and women – differences in genitals and in reproductive capacities. Some writers think that other physical differences like height and secondary sexual characteristics might be added to the list. However, the central point is that *all* differences between the sexes other than these physiological ones are seen as being produced by society.

Gender

Gender refers to all differences between men and women other than the basic physiological ones. It refers to specific social and cultural patterns of behaviour, and to the social characteristics of being a man or a woman in particular historical and social circumstances. Gender is made by society.

There are two other important concepts here, gender identity and sex role. Gender identity refers to a person's self-concept; that is, one's own sense of being male or female. It is useful to contrast this with the idea of sex role, which refers to the patterns of behaviour and the aptitudes and attitudes that society expects from people simply because they are male or female. The causes of gender differences and inequality are the source of much controversy.

The causes of gender inequality: The Nature v. Nurture Debate

The dispute is over the extent to which gender differences are 'natural' and the extent to which they are produced by nurture, in other words by the ways that we bring children up in society. The conservative view states that gender differences and also inequalities based on gender are 'natural', that they are drawn from biological differences, and are an inevitable, unchangeable part of a 'natural order'. Feminist writers, on the other hand, have insisted on the importance of looking critically at gender divisions, which they do not accept as 'natural'. They acknowledge that most societies prescribe different activities and characteristics for males and females, which may come to be seen as 'natural' by the people involved. However, feminists have challenged the 'natural' view and looked for other possible explanations. They assert that the way children are brought up in society is responsible for the vast majority of differences between the genders.

There are biological, social and psychoanalytic theories to explain the process of constructing gender, and we will now go on to look at each of these.

BIOLOGICAL DETERMINISM THEORIES

Biological determinism theories claim that gender differences between males' and females' attitudes, aptitudes and temperaments are primarily the result of biological factors such as chromosomes and hormones. The chromosomes are complex chemical structures contained within each cell of the body. Two of the forty-six chromosomes that humans usually carry in their cells are called the 'sex chromosomes', because they contain among other things the genetic information involved in creating male and female reproductive systems. A female body form is the result if the sex chromosomes are both X, and a male body form if the sex chromosomes are an X and a Y (Birke, 1983). The chromosomes influence the kinds of hormone produced by the body, form the sexual characteristics of the person and determine the physical growth of the two sexes. For the majority of people, chromosomal sex is unambiguous.

Biological determinism theorists assert that chromosomal inheritance is also responsible for the development of gender identity and for sex differences in cognitive skills and personality. 'Sexual and other behaviour differences between men and women occur simply because of differences in male and female hormone secretions . . . this is why men and women think and behave differently' (Verrall, 1979).

Not all scientists agree with these assertions. They point out that we know that male and female bodies produce different quantities of certain hormones. What we do not know is whether they have overriding importance in relation to the individual's subsequent acquisition of gender. Nor is there enough evidence to 'conclude unequivocally that hormones have a major impact on later behaviour', or a determining effect on the development of intellectual and cognitive skills (Birke, 1983, p. 7).

Sociobiology

Sociobiology is the study of social organization in different species including humans, and is another influential perspective in the field of biological determinism. It begins from the view that there is a basic female nature and a basic male nature which draw their characteristics from the facts of different roles in reproduction, rather than simply from chromosomes and hormones. Men's greater physical strength and women's childbearing role generate a division of labour in society, in which both sexes perform distinctive jobs, tasks and roles. This is the underlying cause of the other differences between men and women. It is the natural order, and to maintain harmony society needs to ensure its men are 'manly' and its women remain 'womanly'. Sociobiology thus regards the differences between the genders as in-built, unchangeable and determined by the biology of the two sexes. It also sees them as desirable: Gray, for example, argues that sex differences have a biological basis which cannot and should not be tampered with (Gray, 1981; Goldberg, 1974).

Criticisms of the genetic argument

While we cannot dispute that biologically people differ, it is very difficult to establish categorically the extent to which differences are biological or social in origin. Part of the problem is that biological theories draw heavily on experimental findings from work done on animals, and there are always questions about how far we can extrapolate to humans findings based on animal behaviour.

Biological determinism has difficulty in explaining historical and geographical variations in the position of both sexes. What it means to be a man and what it means to be a woman have both differed greatly across societies. If the distinction were biologically rooted, there should logically be one universal form for each sex (Oakley, 1972; Davidoff, 1973; La Fontaine, 1978). It is also the case that biological explanations cannot adequately account for the effects that socialization has upon the two sexes, nor can they make it clear why socialization is necessary – if sex roles are rooted so firmly in biology, then why bother with all the socialization?

Conclusions

We are not trying to suggest that biology has no influence in creating differences between the genders. However, we cannot ever really know how much effect nature has as opposed to nurture – for one thing it would not be ethical to do the kind of experimentation that would be necessary to find out. What is clear is that there is a continuous process of interaction between social and biological factors in the processes of sex role socialization. A major problem with the biological determinism theories is that they insist that human identity is fixed and unchanging for all time. This can be used to justify both social inequalities and doing nothing to attempt to change or improve a situation which is unfair.

SOCIALIZATION THEORIES

The feminist argument stresses that early socialization rather than biological inheritance is responsible for gender differences in ability and aptitudes.

Socialization

Socialization is defined as 'The process by which an individual learns to be a member of his or her society' (Berger, 1976). It is the way we learn the patterns of thought and behaviour considered acceptable in our society.

These social patterns vary tremendously in different regions, classes and nations. They also vary throughout history; for example, we no longer swaddle babies on the assumption that they will drift apart if we do not, which was the practice and the belief in the Middle Ages.

There are a number of different agents of socialization. The family, other children and teachers are some of the most significant, but the mass media also have a role to play.

Socialization and gender

Early socialization lays down rules about and provides role models for sex-appropriate behaviour and actions (Kelly, 1981; Saraga and Griffiths, 1981). Most societies have patterns of socialization which encourage males to become masculine and females to become feminine. It is clear that there is a series of stages by which the child's understanding grows, and as with other concepts, 'the child's first ideas about sex roles tend to be crude, concrete, oversimplified and exaggerated' (Kelly, 1981, p. 75).

Stages in sex role learning

The child is assigned to a particular gender at birth, and under normal circumstances grows up with that gender identity. The majority of children can label themselves correctly as a boy or a girl by the age of three (Fagot, 1985). They 'usually acquire the concept of gender stability – the notion that gender remains fixed throughout life – within a year or two of acquiring the concept of gender identity'

(Short and Carrington, 1989, p. 23). For a while it seems that young children are not aware that gender is fixed, that it is constant, and may believe that it depends on hairstyle, dress and behaviour rather than on differences in genitals. They may go through a stage of conforming rigidly to the social aspects of sex roles (Kohlberg, 1966). The stage of recognizing gender constancy tends to emerge between the ages of six and seven.

Theories of sex and gender socialization

It is important to acknowledge that we do not at this time have a full explanation of gender socialization. There are a number of different theories on socialization and how it works, which can be divided into two broad groups of social learning theories and cognitive developmental theories.

Social learning theories

Social learning theories suggest that children learn about appropriate attitudes and behaviour from their parents, peers and teachers (Kelly, 1981). The theories can be divided into reinforcement theories and observational theories. Reinforcement theories emphasize the importance of rewards and punishment. Children learn that appropriate behaviour is rewarded, and hence reinforced, while inappropriate behaviour is discouraged or even punished, and is therefore to be avoided. Because children are in a dependent position they want love and approval and so come to accept and repeat what they have been taught (Mischel, 1966). The process works as well for sex role learning as it does for other kinds of socialization. The child is rewarded or punished for sex-appropriate behaviour, and eventually such behaviour becomes second nature.

However, the adult can only reward or punish what the child does. The social learning theorists therefore emphasize the importance of imitation and modelling, since children learn new behaviour by imitating both adults and other children (Bandura, 1971). Another important aspect is that children imitate people whom they see as being like them, so they imitate things that they see same-sex peers and same-sex adults doing.

Assessment of the social learning theories

The main problem with these theories is the extent to which this process of rewarding and punishing children works effectively in fostering desired behaviour. It is anything but an exact science, as anyone with experience of small children will know only too well. It assumes passive children agreeing to all that is said and done to them, which has clear practical problems, but also theoretical ones which we will return to later in the chapter. The other criticisms centre on the degree to which it is true that parents, child-carers and teachers do reward and punish 'gender-appropriate' behaviour. The link between adult behaviour and child sex stereotyping is more often assumed in these theories than demonstrated (Kelly, 1981, p. 76).

Cognitive development theories

Cognitive development theories see the child as motivated primarily by the wish for competence. The theory suggests that children are concerned to develop ways of understanding the world as a means to gaining competence. They develop a number of categories into which they fit their world, and they form rules about the categories. Sex is one of the significant categories they use. In these theories, society presents an image of what is feminine and masculine to children, who then put together a cluster of the attributes that they label as masculine or feminine, and try to copy the appropriate cluster. Cognitive development theories concentrate on learned behaviour which is seen as appropriate for one gender or the other in a particular society (Kelly, 1981).

Assessment of cognitive development theories

Cognitive theories have been developed more recently than social learning ones, and are gaining support. Their main advantage is that the theory conceives of the child as an active participant in structuring her/his experience and formulating sex role concepts. This approach moves away from social learning theory, which sees society as crudely imposing sex role stereotypes upon the individual. Children are regarded as essentially self-socializing; they first develop categories and then fit themselves into the categories.

Conclusions

Although social learning and cognitive development theories are usually presented as competing models of socialization, it is possible to combine both to make a clear and coherent picture. There is research evidence to back up both theories and it is probable that imitation, modelling, reinforcement and cognitive processes all play a part in children's sex role socialization.

PSYCHOANALYTIC THEORIES

We have looked so far at biological and social theories. There are also explanations of the process of gender construction that derive from psychology and specifically from the psychoanalytical traditions. Some writers have suggested that our gender identities and our sexuality are so deep-seated that to understand them thoroughly we need psychoanalytic theory (Mitchell, 1974; Chodorow, 1978). Psychoanalytic theory draws our attention to emotional processes at work within the child and to the psychological dynamics of the family, and considers that we need an account of their complicated structures in order to understand the way our sexual identities are constructed.

The field of psychoanalytic theory is huge; there is not one theory but many competing approaches, and we can provide no more than a brief overview here. Psychoanalytic theories have their roots in the work of Freud, but feminist inspired psychoanalytic theory has in the last few years driven a coach and horses through much of his argument. Psychoanalytic work is largely preoccupied with the early years of life and with the intense feelings and conflicts that confront the growing child. The starting point is the very strong attachment that exists between the child and her/his mother, a bond which is important because of the long period of time that human children are dependent upon their parents. Children are then faced with the job of breaking this attachment and establishing themselves as 'separate' and autonomous individuals. They do this in a series of stages.

Theorists have varying views of this process of separation, but most agree that it is different for boys and girls. Freud argued that the process whereby the boy gives up his first love-object – his mother – is difficult and painful; the child has to resolve a number of feelings which may be only partly conscious. This is the so-called Oedipal conflict. Through it, however, the male child learns to control his desires and his impulses and develops a fully developed social conscience. Girls, in Freud's view, never go through this process; they are seen as failing to mature fully in a psychological sense.

Freud has been attacked for having a 'deficit' view of women. Current psychoanalytic thinking has challenged some of his approach and emphasized femininity in a positive sense, where Freud saw only a negative. The notion of difference and of the complementarity of male and female has been suggested in place of Freud's notion of inferiority and dominance. It has been suggested, too, that boys can be very jealous of girls' femininity, whereas Freud emphasized only that girls envy boys. Our attention has also been drawn to the fact that boys have a more difficult task of growing up in some ways than girls. Skinner and Cleese put it in the following way:

ROBIN   All children normally start with an attachment to the MOTHER
– so I've put them on one side of a metaphorical river. The
father, on the other side, is at first a more distant figure for the
children. To become psychologically male, the boy has got to
'cross the bridge' to be with his FATHER.

JOHN   Whereas the girl can stay where she is with her mother. Cross-
ing the bridge is something extra the boy has to do.

ROBIN   And that means struggling against the powerful mother tie.

(Skinner and Cleese, 1982, p. 248).

This means that boys have to break away from their early identification with their mother and solve the problem of what masculinity is and means. 'For girls, early development is more continuous
and femininity can be easily understood in terms of motherhood'
(Chodorow, 1974). Boys, by contrast, are faced with a constant task of
constructing masculinity. They do this in a number of ways.

Boys need a set of social symbols to signal masculinity. A society
makes categorizations of things that are feminine and things that are
masculine and boys avoid, and perhaps come to dread, any association
with feminine things. In some societies there are very clear distinctions between things that are for men and things that are for women.
In a part of Malaysia, for example, traditionally it is only the men who
ever wear vertical stripes; women wear horizontal ones, and the only
time that horizontal and vertical stripes are mixed is on the covers of
beds for married people.

There is perhaps another, more negative process at work too.
Chodorow also argues that boys try to achieve manhood through a
process of making themselves different and distant from women and
femininity. She suggests that one of the ways they do this is by devaluing and attacking girls and things that are feminine.

Assessment of psychoanalytic theories

It is again important to stress that this is a huge field, and by summing
it up in a few sentences we inevitably oversimplify complex ideas.
Critics of psychoanalytic theory in general are dismissive of the idea
that individuals have an unconscious part of their mind, and are
critical of psychoanalytic theory because it is difficult to test experimentally or 'scientifically'.

However, psychoanalytic ideas have the advantage of focusing on
the emotional aspects of a child's life, and underline the fact that
feelings are involved in the process of gender socialization as well as
the purely cognitive or learning and thinking aspects of the child. The
newer feminist psychoanalytic theories suggest that masculinity is
essentially more 'precarious' than femininity, an idea which takes
us a long way from Freud's deficit model. It has the advantage of
encouraging us to look at the way children use things in the world as
symbols and to try to understand what the symbols mean to children;
it pushes us in the direction of developing a perspective of how
children see the world.

We have aimed to give a brief introduction to the psychological and sociological theories of gender construction and differentiation which have guided and influenced the greater part of research in this area. It is important to emphasize that theories are social constructions; that is, they are only human interpretations and ways of seeing and understanding the world. They are tools, and we need to assess their claims to 'truth' critically.

GENDER CONSTRUCTION AND SCHOOLS

The main theme of this book is the role that schooling plays in the process of gender development, and at the end of this chapter, having looked at the different theories that attempt to explain the processes of gender construction and differentiation, we need to return to this theme. Feminist research is committed to the view that schools do have a role in constructing, defining and reinforcing gender roles and gender identity; it is critical of the role that school plays in gender socialization, and of the ways that schools disadvantage girls. Feminists have attempted to describe the processes by which schools do this. As an introductory comment we can say that they have scrutinized the curriculum, the social and 'moral' ordering of the school and the styles that some teachers adopt. In this book we will look in detail at the issues and practices that they have identified as being important.

We have already commented that we do not as yet have a full account of how gender socialization and differentiation happen. New research is going on, which aims to increase our knowledge of the issues. One area that is important is the work on cognitive development theory. In the light of research evidence from this field, many feminist accounts look to have taken a rather simplistic view of sex role socialization.

These accounts have stressed the different ways in which boys and girls are treated by parents and by schools, and assumed that children simply absorb these differences and repeat them in an identical form. Arnot (1986) has called these approaches 'deterministic'. By this she means that some accounts view the child as passive or 'naked', in the sense of being unaffected by previous experiences and incapable of resisting social pressure. There is no doubt that society does communicate patterns for us to identify with, and that these act as a frame and may constrain our choices. However, what we need to understand is how we come to make individual choices from within that frame, and to build up a 'script' for ourselves.

Other sociological work on schools makes a similar point. Connell (1987) has suggested that we may need a more complex analysis than the one we have. He questions the extent to which schools do transmit a unified gender code. He argues that 'The stereotype argument is seriously wrong in assuming that the school tends to impose just one sex-role pattern on its boys and one pattern on its girls' (1987, p. 42). A range of messages is transmitted and a number of different views of what it means to be a boy or a girl are modelled in school. In addition, pupils are exposed to several agencies of socialization, which probably transmit a range of different gender codes. Skeggs (1989) points out that some of the socialization theorists have assumed all these agencies propagate an identical set of messages.

Pupils, then, choose elements from this gender code and mix them with ideas that derive from their own background and community culture. Wolpe is in agreement with this view, commenting, 'Overall there is a great deal going on in a classroom at any one time, and a complex set of contradictory messages are simultaneously being generated' (Wolpe, 1989, p. 45). Again we get a picture of a more complex and contradictory process at work than was suggested in some of the earlier theories. Anyon (1983) and Skeggs (1986) have shown through their research that children reflect, rework and challenge some of the aspects of the gender code they are given: they do not simply absorb them intact.

Any analysis which takes socialization as the main factor producing sex-based differences in education has other limitations (Arnot, 1986). Socialization cannot explain why gender has developed in the way it has. Neither can socialization theories explain why gender codes change over time. We need, in the view of some feminist authors, to add in a political economy perspective to the analysis. They suggest that we need a picture of the social and economic conditions and the prevalent images of femininity and masculinity in which schools operate in order to understand the processes of gender differentiation and inequality in education. Recent studies have examined the history of the state's education and other social policies to develop a sense of how sex role ideologies and girls' role in schools change over time (Dyhouse, 1977; David, 1978; Davin, 1978; Purvis, 1981a).

We may need to develop more subtle and complex understandings of what goes on in our schools if we are to be able to intervene in the processes by which girls are disadvantaged there. The family, home, community and media obviously play important parts in gender socialization. Schools and teachers do so too – although this is not always consciously acknowledged. And it is the case that children themselves play an active part in matching their behaviour to, and living up to, gender stereotypes. Davies (B. Davies, 1989) makes us aware of how pre-school children actively seek to take their place in the world, and of how an appropriate gender role is a central element for them. We want to suggest that if equal opportunities are to be advanced, it is necessary to make this process explicit, to encourage and help students and teachers to reflect critically on what they are doing and on the implications of their actions, and to make more conscious choices about what they wish to do in schools.

CONCLUSIONS

We live in a society in which there is substantial inequality, and some of this inequality is based on gender. There are a number of competing explanations for this situation, and considerable controversy exists between the different explanations. The starting point is the fact that not everyone agrees that gender inequality is a problem. Feminists challenge the status quo on the grounds that it is unjust, but they are by no means in a majority. There is still considerable debate and political heat in this question, and much of the writing that appears in the field is polemical and politically charged. It is not a debate which is over and settled, but one which continues to generate controversy, not least in schools at the moment, where the issue of equal opportunities for girls is now on the political agenda.

CHAPTER SUMMARY

In this chapter we introduce the main themes and aims of the book. We look at the facts of women's inequality in society and in the education system. We introduce some of the concepts that are important in this field, like the distinction between sex and gender. We also discuss the biological, sociological and psychological theories of the formation of gender. We review the significance that gender has for education and for the experience of schooling.

SUGGESTIONS FOR FURTHER READING

Sex and gender

Lloyd, B. and Archer, J. (1976) *Exploring Sex Differences*. London: Academic Press.
Oakley, A. (1972) *Sex, Gender and Society*. London: Temple Smith. This book provides a good introduction.

Issues of sexual anatomy and gender confusion

Kessler, S. and McKenna, W. (1985) *Gender: An Ethno-methodological Approach*. Chicago: University of Chicago Press. Chapter 2 has a detailed discussion.

Laquer, T. (1990) *Making Sex, Body and Gender: From the Greeks to Freud*. Cambridge, MA: Harvard University Press.

Definitions of masculinity and femininity

There is a substantial body of material which shows the different ways that masculinity and femininity have been defined in different cultures and in different times in history.

Davidoff, L. (1973) *The Best of Circles*. London: Croom Helm. This book looks at historical evidence.

La Fontaine, J.S. (1978) *Sex and Age as Principles of Social Differentiation*. London: Academic Press. This book looks at anthropological evidence.

Mead, M. (1950) *Male and Female*. Harmondsworth: Penguin.

The nature v. nurture debate

Birke, L. (1983) Nature and culture. Units 2 and 3 of *U221, The Changing Experience of Women*. Milton Keynes: Open University Press. This deals with the nature v. nurture debate in a full but concise way.

Brighton Women and Science Group (eds) (1980) *Alice through the Microscope: The Power of Science over Women's Lives*. London: Virago. This deals with issues of women and science including biological determinism and sociobiology.

Hutt, C. (1972) *Males and Females*. Harmondsworth: Penguin.

Psychological theories of gender formation

Maccoby, E.E. and Jacklin, C.N. (1974) *The Psychology of Sex Differences*. Stanford: Stanford University Press.

Sayers, J. (1987) Psychology and gender divisions. In G. Weiner and M. Arnot (eds), *Gender under Scrutiny: New Inquiries in Education*. London: Hutchinson.

Women's inequality in society

Reid, I. and Stratta, E. (eds) (1989) *Sex Differences in Britain*. Aldershot: Gower. This provides a useful review of the different kinds of inequality that women face in society. The basic assumption is that men and women have different levels of access to almost all social resources, power positions and opportunities, which all work to the disadvantage of women. The figures are up to date.

Gender and school

Delamont, S. (1990) *Sex Roles and the School*. London: Routledge. This book is a useful introduction to the issues of gender and schooling.

Marland, M. (1983) *Sex Differentiation in Schooling*. London: Heinemann.

CHAPTER 2

Feminist theories

CHAPTER OVERVIEW

There are many different perspectives within feminism. The three most familiar are liberal, socialist and radical feminism. In this chapter we try to establish the main points of each and clarify the ways they relate to established traditions of political thought. We also trace the approach to education that each of these different perspectives has taken. Two other feminist perspectives are psychoanalytic and post-modernist feminism. They are much less well known, and as they have less immediate relevance to education, we look much more briefly at the first of them, and provide only references for the second. Lastly we look at the study of 'masculinities' that has developed recently.

Feminism is not one theory, but has many different perspectives within it. Feminism is usually divided into three main categories, liberal feminism, radical feminism and socialist feminism. However, in recent years psychoanalytic theories of feminism have become important and post-modernism is also beginning to develop an influence.

There are some similarities between all of the theories. What unites them is the emphasis they place on how central gender divisions are to the way a society works. Feminism starts from the position that the ways that women are treated are unfair, and is based on a commitment to a political project – to developing strategies of change in order to create full rights and opportunities for women. It is important to note that the different perspectives are not only significant at a theoretical level; they also affect views of what should be done. In the last chapter of this book we look at the way that the different feminist approaches affect strategies for change within education.

The issues which distinguish the different approaches from each other can be organized into three areas:

1 The causes of women's oppression, and the importance they give to 'patriarchy'.
2 The programme for change.
3 The ultimate goal for society.

PATRIARCHY

We looked in Chapter 1 at a number of concepts and ideas that have been important in feminist writing. Patriarchy is another significant concept, with a central role in the disagreements between different feminist theories.

Patriarchy

There are differences between men and women in society, and it is important to look at the way these differences are ranked and to recognize that these differences make for powerful forms of inequality. This involves an examination of power and politics. In all the societies which have been reliably studied, males have more power and authority than females, and specifically they have power over females. The degree and the character of their power vary considerably and there is no universal pattern. Men and women are not just different, but are in a power relationship with each other.

Some men can exercise more power than others, but patriarchy emphasizes the benefits that come to all men from the domestic labour and sexual subordination of women.

There is in fact a great deal of controversy over what the term patriarchy means, and we will discuss this in more detail later in the chapter, but it is important to note that it implies a hierarchy of social relations and institutions through which men are able to dominate women, and also men who are younger or who have less power.

In this chapter we need to try to establish the main points of each of the feminist theories, to clarify the ways in which they relate to established traditions of political thought, and to indicate the effect they have each had upon the study of education. We will not deal with post-modernist feminism, for it has yet to have much influence on the feminist analysis of education, although post-modernism is beginning to have an effect more generally in the field of sociology of education (Ball, 1990; Walkerdine, 1984, for work on discourse in child-centred education theory; B. Davies, 1989, and Calder, forthcoming, for a post-structuralist account of early years' education).

LIBERAL FEMINISM

Liberal feminism is based upon the political philosophy of liberalism. Liberalism starts from a belief in the rights of the individual as based essentially on the fact of the individual's humanity, but also on the individual's capacity for rationality. All individuals have rights to freedom and autonomy and to a voice in how they are governed. Liberal feminism appeals to the central principles of liberty, equality and fairness for all to justify women's rights.

Liberalism first emerged as a political force in the seventeenth century in Britain. The first feminist statements based on the philosophy were made a little later. In the *Vindication of the Rights of Women*, written in 1792, Wollstonecraft argued that women have as much potential as men, but are stunted by being reared to fit an image of weakness and femininity, and degraded by having always to please men. Women need to be offered the same civil liberties and the same economic opportunities as men in order to develop their true potential.

John Stuart Mill in the nineteenth century developed these ideas further, arguing that equal rights for women are necessary to remedy the injustice done to them. Moreover, these rights are also essential to promote the whole moral and intellectual progress of humanity. Women's inequality is unfair, and must be remedied if the goals of liberalism are to be realized for the society as a whole.

What is to be done: the liberal feminist programme for change

Today liberal feminists emphasize the fact that all men and women should have equal rights and that any legal or social constraints that block the achievements and development of talented individuals from whatever gender, class or race should be abolished. Their programmes for change are set by their belief that individuals should have occupations and positions that are based on their ability and nothing else. Liberal feminists place reliance on legal remedies, and have taken up the cause of legal reform to ensure that women have equal opportunities with men. Women are urged to take up opportunities offered to them and to realize their full potential at work and in public as well as private life.

Criticisms of liberal feminism

Liberal feminists are criticized on much the same basis as liberalism itself, namely that they overemphasize individual freedom at the expense of the needs of the community. There is a limit to what the individual can achieve, and her/his rights must be reconciled with those of others in the community. Other feminists suggest that the view of the self as a rational, autonomous individual which is at the heart of liberalism is in itself a very male view of the way people and society work.

Socialist feminists are critical of liberal feminism for its emphasis on formal legal rights and the provision of equal opportunities. They allege that this programme fails to tackle the problems of poverty and economic oppression which prevent women and other deprived groups from taking advantage of opportunities.

Other feminists, particularly black feminists, have suggested that liberal feminism is a middle-class white movement. They have claimed that it is little more than a self-improvement programme, which encourages women to compete for top jobs and live by the same values as men. 'Instead of the sexy chick or the perfect home-maker, we now have a new image to live up to; the liberated woman' (E. Willis, 1975, p. 170). The problem is that this is only relevant to an elite and ignores the difficulties of many women from disadvantaged groups in society.

Radical feminists argue that liberal feminism, which views men as fellow victims of sex role conditioning, fails to recognize the power men have over women in a patriarchal society. They also allege that liberal feminists want women to become more like men, and that their goal for society is a system in which women can compete with men and behave like them.

Education and liberal feminism

Education has always been important for liberals, who are committed to the view that it replaces ignorance and prejudice by knowledge and enlightenment. They started from a belief that education allows the individual to attain self-fulfilment and develop their potential to the full. Wollstonecraft and Mill both emphasized the importance of education for the emancipation of women. Early liberals worked to establish provision of education for girls and their rights of access to educational institutions. Later the issue of developing a legal framework to ensure equality of access and equal opportunity in educational settings became important too.

Assessment and conclusions

It is important to note that much contemporary feminist thought defines itself in reaction to liberal feminism. More radical thinkers have been critical of its reform orientation, denying that any important change can be achieved under the existing political and social system. However, liberal ideas and values have been the basis for all central political and legal reforms achieved in the last hundred years, so their achievements should not be trivialized. Educational and legal reforms to increase women's professional and occupational rights are still not complete, there are still areas of discrimination, and not all the gains are yet secure. Liberal principles still have scope and power in the public mind to uphold feminist claims.

SOCIALIST FEMINISM

Socialist feminism is an umbrella term, and a number of different approaches are included in this category. The most important differences between them are the extent to which each accepts the principles of Marxism.

Marxism

The political philosophy of Marxism developed in the nineteenth century and grew from Marx's own experience and view of industrialization. The Marxist perspective argues that inequality is the result of the economic, social and political structures in which people live. Marx started from a 'materialist' idea of society, and from the concept of the 'mode of production'. The mode of production refers to two things: forces of production and the 'relations of production' – that is, the way in which production is organized by people. In western industrialized nations the system is capitalism, which is responsible for exploitation and inequality. Other economic systems produce different patterns of inequality.

This material 'base' of a society generates a 'superstructure'. The superstructure is the layer of legal, social and political agencies and institutions that have power in that society, and the social, political and legal ideas that dominate in the society. Education can be seen as an important agent in the superstructure.

Marxism and women

Marx has little to say that is specific to women; women's oppression is simply part of the inequality produced by the capitalist system. Other Marxists have looked at the role of the family in generating women's inequality in capitalist society. Engels suggested that as private property grew in importance the family changed its character, and women became more oppressed. The growth of capitalism meant an enormous growth in the significance of private property and succeeded in obliterating any equality that had existed in the human community.

What is to be done: the Marxist programme for change

In the Marxist view the working class, which is oppressed by capitalism, must make a revolution to liberate themselves. There is no possibility of reforming the system peacefully or gradually. Capitalism must be replaced with a socialist system in which the means of production belong to one and all. The oppression of women will disappear simultaneously, as it is part of class inequality.

Criticisms of Marxism

The Marxist analysis of society and history is highly controversial, in this chapter we consider only the feminist view of Marxism. A number of feminist groups have criticized Marxism for being 'gender blind', and for its 'silences' about the position of women and their subordination.

Socialist feminism and Marxism

Socialist feminists have tried to take account of this criticism while holding on to the basic insights that Marxism offers. They acknowledge the importance of material factors in the oppression of women, but do not see that living in a class society is the only source or even the primary source of women's oppression. Socialist feminism suggests that both patriarchy and capitalism have to be taken account of, and that both must be defeated.

What is to be done: the Socialist Feminist programme for change

Socialist and Marxist feminists share a belief that only limited change can be achieved within the capitalist system. This is the main point of difference with liberal feminists. However, socialist feminists have pressed for change within the present system, concentrating on the issue of women's participation in the workforce, and on the state welfare support system which discriminates systematically against women.

Women's participation in the labour force is determined by the division of labour. Since the development of capitalism, they are not considered as being primarily engaged in productive, waged work outside the home. They do unpaid domestic labour, look after children, men and the old in our society, and hence reproduce the next generation of workers. The domestic work that women do is not seen as being as important as the work that men do outside the home, and this contributes to their subordinate status. One programme for action has been to suggest that the status of domestic labour could be improved if women were paid wages for housework (Dalla Costa and James, 1972).

When women do enter waged work, they tend to be poorly qualified and skilled, because it is not seen as their main 'job'. This also contributes to their lack of status in society. Socialist feminists argue that women's position could be greatly enhanced by their achieving a greater degree of equality with men in the public sphere. They share this objective with the liberal feminists, but not their optimism that change can be easily achieved by the passing of equal opportunities legislation and greater knowledge and awareness on the part of employers. Socialist feminists assume that the process of women gaining equality in the work place will create conflict, and will require a struggle.

The socialist feminist programme has tried to take account of the needs of disadvantaged groups in society. It recognizes that many women currently work in the lowest paid, unskilled jobs, and that it is therefore essential to strengthen their unionization and press for better pay and conditions. Socialist feminism has also underlined the inadequacies and injustices of social welfare services. It is the most disadvantaged women who are dependent on these services, and socialist feminists have campaigned for changes in the way they work.

Criticisms of socialist feminism

Liberal feminists have criticized socialist feminists for going too far in challenging a system which they believe does not need to be changed in any fundamental way, but merely fine-tuned to redress a balance for women. Radical feminists have criticized socialist feminism for not going far enough. In their view socialist feminists continue to emphasize the significance of social structure and capitalism in the oppression of women, and fail to give enough space to patriarchy. Radical feminists argue that if Marxism or socialism is to ensure the liberation of women it must further incorporate some understanding of patriarchy as an incredibly powerful and tenacious system, which intersects with capitalism but is separate from it.

Radical feminists have also criticized socialist feminists for making the economic well-being and independence of women their main concern. Non-Marxist feminists believe that this is simplistic and that it misses out on a large area of women's oppression. They question whether a change in women's work and economic status is enough to change women's position in society.

Education and socialist feminism

Marxist and socialist feminists have looked critically at the role that education systems play in creating and justifying social inequalities. We will outline the arguments here and examine them in more detail in Chapters 5 and 6.

Reproduction of inequality through education

We have already discussed the fact that most sociologists recognize that schools are a sophisticated mechanism for selection. Marxist sociologists take the view that the main role of schooling is to transmit inequality between the generations. The selection procedures ensure that the class structure is reproduced from one generation to the next. In addition they ensure that the values that are necessary for the capitalist system to function are transmitted to children. Education in the Marxist view is an important agent in 'reproducing' the capitalist system (Althusser, 1971; Bowles and Gintis, 1976).

Socialist feminists have drawn attention to the role that gender plays, arguing that schools reproduce both gender inequality and class inequality. They suggest that class and gender are connected to each other and so interwoven that it is theoretically difficult to draw them apart. Working-class girls are in a doubly disadvantaged position in schools; they undergo the same experience of class inequality as their male counterparts, but they also receive messages about their subordination to men. The division of labour is a crucial factor in socialist feminists' thinking. They suggest that schools direct a range of messages about appropriate roles and activities to girls and thereby occupy a central place in reproducing the division of labour across the generations.

Winning consent

In recent years Marxist scholarship has moved away from a purely 'determinist' position. Marxist sociologists have argued that schools do not simply force or coerce people into a subordinate role, but rather manage to win consent for the allocation process (Willis, 1977). In school, everyone is seen to have had a fair chance, and talented children do well and leave the others behind. In this way education convinces people that it is fair that they occupy the place to which they have been assigned.

Gender is involved here too. Socialist feminists suggest that schools play a part in gaining the consent of girls to their subordinate status and to their place in the domestic sphere. Schools are also involved in winning the consent of boys to a definition of masculinity which makes them primarily responsible for the economic support of the family.

Resistance

However, 'winning consent' is not a simple task, and it is not accomplished without struggle. One of the issues that is important for Marxists and socialist feminists is that children, and working-class children in particular, do not passively accept the socialization process that is happening to them in schools. They try to resist what is going on, which leads Marxists to a particular interest in the forms of rebellion and deviance that occur in schools. Socialist feminist research has shown that girls have different forms of rebellion and resistance from boys. Resistance seems to have different meanings for them, and a different significance for the process of reproduction of gender differentiation and class inequalities.

Marxist sociology has described the processes involved in producing and reinforcing social class inequality. The argument is therefore at first sight very different from the liberal feminist one, which sees education as a liberating agent and a force for good. However, socialist and Marxist feminism shares this view of the potential that education has to benefit society and the individual; but they emphasize that the way it operates in our society prevents working-class children from receiving those benefits.

Assessment and conclusions

Socialist feminism and Marxist feminism have drawn our attention to the importance of social structure and class in the patterns of inequality in our society. While acknowledging that we need to know about gender discrimination in school, socialist feminists insist that we cannot fully understand the problem without taking account of the whole social context and the class system. They argue that the strategies of both liberal and radical feminists cannot in themselves achieve really significant change. This is because they cannot have any significant effect on the division of labour at the workplace or in the home. Only a wholesale change in the way capitalism operates can do that.

RADICAL FEMINISM

Radical feminism is a perspective which is still evolving and changing. Much of the writing of the 1970s and 1980s which originated from this section of the women's movement cannot be classified in terms of existing political theories. It is new and original and, as its name suggests, radical. There are two key ideas in radical feminism: firstly that patriarchy is of overarching importance, and secondly that the personal is political.

Radical feminism asserts that it is patriarchy that oppresses women, and that their subordination stems from the social, economic and political dominance of men in society. It is men who have forced women into oppressed situations and functions. Women's domination is therefore the deepest and strongest form of inequality, and the most difficult to eradicate.

In contrast to the socialist writers, radical feminists argue that patriarchy must override all other forms of inequality. Radical feminists point to the fact that women are oppressed by men and in a worse position than men whatever the economic and political system of society. They are critical of socialist feminists for the stress they place on class oppression. Radical feminists attack liberal feminism, on the other hand, for its failure to recognize the power of men, and for its assumption that those who have power will voluntarily give it up.

For radical feminists relationships between men and women are governed by patriarchy. Personal and sexual relationships reflect those power relationships, are tainted by the deep power imbalance, and therefore need to be changed. Sexuality has become a crucial issue for radical feminists, and they have emphasized that men aim to control women's sexuality. They have focused on different varieties of male sexual domination – pornography, prostitution, sexual harassment and violence against women – and have been prepared to fight politically against these issues and problems in our society.

Radical feminism has also been critical of the family, since it too is permeated by patriarchy. Greer, for example, saw the nuclear family living isolated in its own individual home as a prison (Greer, 1981). There have been demands for the abolition of the nuclear family, and attempts made to create alternative communal structures.

Initially radical feminists were preoccupied with the enslaving aspects of women's biology and psychology, and were concerned to minimize differences between men and women: androgyny was the ideal. They accepted implicitly that traditional masculine pursuits were superior to traditional female ones like child-rearing and domestic work and consequently they rejected the traditional female role. This approach has been changing in recent years, with the development of the idea that a feminist revolution must mean more than women simply imitating men. This led to a re-evaluation of the traditional values of femininity and the talents of women. Radical feminists have come to view women's biology, especially their reproductive capacities and the nurturant personality that they believe derives from it, as a potential source of liberation for women. If men can adopt some of the characteristics that are now seen as female there is hope for change throughout society.

27

What is to be done: the radical feminist programme for change

In the radical feminist view, existing legal and political structures must be abolished to achieve women's emancipation. The programme is a radical one; social and cultural institutions need fundamental revision, and the family is an especially important agency for the reform of personal lives.

However, individuals too must be prepared to make sweeping changes, as significant areas of personal life need to be restructured. Women will always be subordinate to men unless sexuality and the forms of sexual relations between the sexes are changed. Radical feminists therefore call for an end to patriarchal structures, but also insist that women must take more control over their own lives, and refuse to bow to the power of men. The most extreme radical feminists advocate a complete separation of the sexes. They believe that a complete commitment to feminism means becoming lesbian, and perhaps separatist. They engage in total non-co-operation with men, believing that only with their own institutions can women really find freedom.

This is a very different approach from liberal feminism, where men are seen as fellow victims and each sex can be liberated by education, legal change and good will. It also stands in great contrast to socialist feminists, who wish men and women to fight together to bring change from a system that oppresses them both.

Some radical feminist writers feel that inequality between men and women is rooted basically in the nature of human reproductive biology. For most feminists this has meant demanding access to contraception and abortion as a basic right for women. Firestone (1979) went further. She argued that until there is some new technological way of reproducing the human species, which frees women from pregnancy and childbirth, then women will not be able to be fully liberated.

Radical feminists do not see that it is possible to change social and political institutions by legislation and piecemeal reform, since men will not give up the power they have willingly or easily. Legislation cannot eradicate sexual inequality anyway. A transfer of power to the working class will not necessarily liberate women either. What is needed is a transfer of power from men to women. Radical feminists emphasize that this means that struggle is necessary to change the way society works. Patriarchy can never be reformed in the radical feminist view; instead it must be ripped out root and branch.

Criticisms of radical feminism

Radical feminist accounts emphasize the role of male power as universally important; radical feminists therefore fail to distinguish between various forms of male power, or between different classes and types of men, who have varying amounts of power. They ignore issues of 'race' and class, and the fact that not all men have equal ability to oppress all women. Moreover, radical feminists can tend towards an assumption that the female nature is all 'good' and that male nature is essentially bad. This means they see all men as victimizers who are by nature incapable of being anything other than exploitative.

Education and radical feminism

The radical feminists' account of education is concerned to analyse the way patriarchy spreads its web in schools, and has concentrated on the power relationships between boys and girls there. They suggest that boys dominate schools and classrooms and that this has a very negative effect on girls' chances of success at school. Boys are seen as a major source, although not the sole one, of the problems that girls have in school. The general argument is that boys dominate classrooms and take the lion's share of the teacher's attention. Their interests dominate the curriculum and leave girls out. Teachers have to concentrate on boys, and the way teachers treat girls in comparison with the boys works to lower the self-esteem of girls.

The other issue for radical feminists is that of sexual harassment. They argue that there is a good deal of sexual harassment of girls in school by both fellow pupils and male teachers. Mahony considers that 'Boys spend an enormous amount of time and energy in the social control of girls. A great deal of what is said by boys to girls constitutes verbal abuse and all girls suffer some form of harassment in school' (Mahony, 1985, p. 53).

In this analysis, boys have the power to reduce girls' chances of success at school. Girls do not 'retire gracefully from academic competition', but rather are pushed out by being treated negatively by the boys. Boys behave as if girls as a category are laughable and may become even more so as they mature. This may go some way towards explaining the polarization and voluntary segregation of girls from boys which characterizes the late phase of schooling (Shaw, 1980, p. 73). The suggestion is that girls withdraw from the danger zones in schools, where their presence simply invites abuse. The boys' sexism therefore shapes the image the girls have of their future lives.

Assessment and conclusions

Liberal and socialist feminists argue that if we look in detail at the daily working of the school classroom, then there are problems in substantiating the radical feminist analysis. There is great variety in the way that boys behave, and not all are confident enough to oppress girls (Connell, 1989). Wolpe comments that we have very little research on the ordinary boy who goes through schooling doing minimal work but not domineering or sexually abusing or harassing girls (Wolpe, 1989, p. 92). Recent research by Troyna and Hatcher documents the fact that there is also more resistance on the part of at least some girls to the boys' oppressive behaviour than is suggested in some of the feminist accounts (L. Davies, 1984, gives many examples; see also Troyna and Hatcher, 1992).

The radical feminist analysis has brought issues of reproduction, sexuality and children's socialization into the debate about women's rights. It has therefore enlarged the debate and moved it away from issues of work, status and public life, which both liberal and socialist feminists had dwelt upon. It has allowed a re-evaluation of femininity and the characteristics of empathy, caring and nurturing which are usually defined as feminine, and it has stressed the importance of the support and warmth that women can and do offer to each other.

PSYCHOANALYTIC FEMINISM

We have given an account of psychoanalytic theories of gender social-ization and gender formation in children in Chapter 1. Our intention here is to provide an account of the way gender inequality develops later in life and to link that material with education.

One of the important issues for psychoanalytic feminism is sex-uality and particularly female sexuality. They start from an assertion that we live in a society which has many taboos on sexuality in general, but women's sexuality in particular. Through the process of gender socialization girls learn guilt and confusion about their sexual feelings, and this means their sexuality does not develop fully. In a sense girls' sexuality is taken away from them, they are dispossessed of it.

Psychoanalytic feminism asserts that the oppression of women affects their emotional life and sexuality as well as their place in the work force and institutions of society. In this way psychoanalytic feminism is like radical feminism in that it draws our attention to private as opposed to public areas of life.

What is to be done: the psychoanalytic feminist programme for change

Psychoanalytic feminists find the roots of women's oppression embedded deep in the emotional psyche. Mitchell, for example, emphasizes that in order for women to free themselves, an 'interior' revolution is necessary. This is not to deny the reality of social, economic and legal disadvantages which every woman faces, but it is to insist that 'she must do more than fight for her rights as a citizen, she must also probe the depths of her psyche' (Mitchell, 1974). In a sense Mitchell sees women as colluding with men; they allow men to be dominant, therefore women need to challenge their own oppression. She acknowledges that this will be a difficult and painful process.

The other change that can affect future generations lies in child-rearing practices. Psychoanalytic feminists suggest that a number of changes in the child-rearing practices of modern society are advisable. Chodorow, in particular, is convinced that mothers dominate child-rearing and that this is the source of a great many problems in the emotional make-up of the individual, and has argued for more fathers to become deeply involved in child-care (Chodorow, 1978).

Criticisms of psychoanalytic feminism

Other feminists criticize psychoanalytic feminism for underplaying the significance that economic, social and legal factors have for women's position in the family and society. This material oppression makes it very difficult for women to reflect critically on their individual and social position. Nevertheless, psychoanalytic feminism has the advantage of drawing our attention to the way that oppression is experienced by each individual, and to how it feels.

Education and psychoanalytic feminism

At first sight it may not seem that these theories have a great deal to do with what goes on inside the schools of the western industrial world, but they have been used to explain some of the processes at work there. The first issue is that of sexuality. Schools are involved in gender socialization, and therefore communicate messages about the nature of sexuality. If they do not do this 'officially', then at least the hidden curriculum has a role.

The second set of ideas that has direct relevance is of those that deal with gender identity. We noted in Chapter 1 that psychoanalytic theories suggest that males and females use a set of symbols to signal gender identity. When boys come into contact with girls in mixed schools it is likely that there will be a division between them according to interests, activities and aspirations. Boys and girls in schools will choose to do and be very different things from each other as a way of signalling that they are male or female. This may help us understand what happens in relation to curriculum choice, when boys choose the sciences and girls choose the arts and domestic sciences. Adolescence is the time when sex role differentiation is at its most intense, 'when pupils are consumed with a concern to establish themselves as feminine or masculine' (Measor, 1984, p. 173). As Kelly puts it, 'Each sex when educated with the other is at puberty almost driven by developmental changes to use subject preference and where possible subject choice as a means of ascribing its sex role' (Kelly, 1981, p. 102). The constant presence of the other sex creates pressure to maintain boundaries, distinctiveness and identity, in Shaw's view (1980). Subject choice and different activities in schools may be a very useful resource for adolescents at this stage in their lives.

Assessment and conclusions

Psychoanalytic feminism can therefore be seen as complementary to liberal and socialist feminist ideas and concerns. Where the latter emphasize the importance of social factors or the struggle for legal rights and equal access to public life, the psychoanalytic approach emphasizes internal and emotional issues, and indicates the sense in which women do have some power to bring about change.

MASCULINITIES

In the last few years a new area of study of gender has been developing. A number of men, mostly starting from a Marxist perspective, have become interested in the study of 'masculinities'. They begin from a concern about the inequalities of power between men and women, and the injustices of patriarchy. Hearn (1987), for example, writes that men exact a human 'tithe' from women, which they take directly and without any recompense. He suggests that the main principle governing the lives of women is their pervasive powerlessness in relation to men, and he recognizes that this is expressed most clearly in the area of sexuality and sexual relationships.

Those researching masculinity are aware that social and economic change has created pressure for alterations in the way masculinity is defined. Factors like widespread unemployment and the decline of traditional industrial settings have had an effect, as has the growth of the welfare state, which has eroded the amount of power that men enjoyed within the family.

Writers on masculinity concentrate on the price that men have had to pay for the power they have. They lament the fact that 'The nurturing and gentler side of men has been obscured through the socialisation process' (Hearn, 1987, p. 11). They consider that there is now an opportunity to change the power differential between men and women, and in the process for men to rediscover the 'shadow' side of their natures. However, this will not be an easy matter. Hearn draws up the balance sheet:

> The pessimism lies in men's remorseless and potential domination at almost all times and in almost all spheres. The optimism jumps out from

the fact that men can be different, can be loving, sharing, caring and intimate. (Hearn, 1987, p. xi).

Assessment and conclusions

The study of masculinities is an interesting new development, which has the advantage of presenting the meaning of masculinity from the 'inside'. At the moment the work is confined to a small audience, and has little chance to create widespread change. It is also the case that much of the fabric of the study of masculinities does seem to be built upon the work and the insights of feminism, and in a sense therefore is parasitic upon feminism.

CONCLUSIONS

There are major differences between the different feminist groups in their approaches, understandings and goals for the future. However, there is much that is shared as well. In terms of education it is clear that, despite the differences and the difficulties, the feminist movement has succeeded in making girls 'visible' in the research on schools, for previously a great number of studies had only researched boys. The work that feminists have done has got the issue of discrimination against girls on to an official agenda and into the minds of teachers and education policy-makers.

It is possible to argue that the attempt to create distinct boundaries between the different categories of feminist thought and the different groups is artificial. It is difficult to place particular writers in categories and to put a label on them. McFadden (1984) has argued that dividing feminism up in this way is unhelpful. What we need is new categories which will allow for more open-endedness and fluidity, and which recognize the overlaps and the connections that exist between different groups and individuals. Tong concludes, 'All of these perspectives cannot be equally correct, but each have made a rich and lasting contribution to feminist thought, and feminist thought is still growing and changing' (Tong, 1988, p. 237).

CHAPTER SUMMARY

This chapter has looked at the different feminist perspectives. Liberal feminism believes women are oppressed in so far as they suffer unjust discrimination as a result of legal and social constraints. The remedy therefore lies in legal measures to remove these constraints and in education to change the social attitudes. Marxists and socialist feminists believe that women are oppressed because of their exclusion from public production, and because of the exploitation of the capitalist

system. The remedy lies in women entering the world of waged work, although the solution lies only in a wholesale change in the system. Radical feminists see women's oppression as resting mainly in the universal control that men exercise over society and over women. The remedy lies in changing patriarchal attitudes and in encouraging women to take more power over their own lives.

Liberal feminism encourages all women to make full use of all their opportunities in education, and fights for a programme of legal reform of any discriminatory practices in the education system. Socialist and radical feminism are both interested in more radical programmes of change in schools to lessen and finally abolish inequalities and to encourage resistance and change in the social structure in which schooling is set.

SUGGESTIONS FOR FURTHER READING

Theories of feminism

Carter, A. (1988) *The Politics of Women's Rights*. London: Longman. This is an accessible introduction to feminism. It has a useful chapter which gives a short account of the different perspectives in feminism, although it does not relate them to education.

Mason, N. and Jewson, D. (1986) The theory and practice of equal opportunities policies: liberal and radical approaches. *The Sociological Review*, **34** (2), 307–34. An interesting article which looks at some of the theoretical underpinning of the different ideas within this field.

Tong, R. (1988) *Feminist Thought: A Comprehensive Introduction*. London: Unwin Hyman. Another reasonably accessible account, with more detail about the different feminist perspectives, and useful sections relating them to existing political theories. It does not relate the theories to the education system.

Patriarchy

The concept of patriarchy has produced debate which we cannot go into here. It tends to be a highly theoretical debate, and none of the material is written in an introductory way. Tong and Carter both deal with the subject.

Beechey, V. (1979) On patriarchy. *Feminist Review* (3), 66–82.

Millett, K. (1971) *Sexual Politics*. London: Rupert Hart-Davis.

Rowbotham, S. (1979) The trouble with patriarchy. *New Statesman*, vol. **98**.

Walby, S. (1985) *Patriarchy at Work*. Cambridge: Polity Press.

Masculinities

Hearn, G. (1987) *The Gender of Oppression*. Brighton: Harvester Wheatsheaf.

CHAPTER 3

Historical background and legislation

CHAPTER OVERVIEW

Our aim in this chapter is to take a brief look at the history of the education and schooling of girls and boys. If we are to understand the present we need to have some idea about what happened in the past, because even though cause and effect are rarely simple and straightforward, what happened then lays the foundations for what happens now.

In the first part of the chapter we focus on the development of schooling for girls in the late nineteenth and early twentieth centuries. We consider the schooling of middle- and working-class girls and the growth of the state sector. We then move on to discuss some of the implications that major education acts and reports up to the 1988 Education Reform Act have had for girls in state schools.

A GENDERED CURRICULUM PRE-1870

What is deemed to be appropriate education and schooling for girls and boys is closely tied up with prevalent notions of femininity and masculinity and with the sexual division of labour. Up until the late nineteenth century a large proportion of working-class children and the majority of middle-class girls received their education – that is, their preparation for life – in the home and in a 'family' setting. Whether they were working- or middle-class, educated at school or at home, what girls learnt was usually heavily oriented towards their future female role. Even apparently 'neutral' areas carried different messages for girls and boys, and for girls and boys of different classes.

For the vast majority of girls the stress was on domesticity and on serving and servicing men, who, they were taught explicitly and implicitly, were superior in physical, moral, intellectual and social terms.

There were, of course, exceptions. For example, from around the fourth century AD convents had offered women an alternative to marriage and childbirth. In many convents, as well as praying and meditating, nuns were involved in studying such subjects as religion, medicine and science, in learning and reading Latin, in composing and making music, in calligraphy and in other artistic and intellectual activities. They also took in pupils from noble families.

In the seventeenth century a very small minority of wealthy Catholic families flouted the law which made schools where the Catholic religion was taught illegal and sent their daughters to schools founded by Mary Ward, an English nun. In these schools the curriculum incorporated 'Latin, science, mathematics, philosophy, modern languages, literature, drama, music and painting and a form of debating called disputation' [Bennett and Forgan, 1991, p. 19]. These girls were learning that it was possible for women to study for their own personal development. However, they were extremely few in number, and if they left school rather than staying on and becoming nuns many of them, no doubt, found limited scope to pursue their interests.

THE DEVELOPMENT OF SCHOOLING FOR GIRLS IN THE LATE NINETEENTH AND EARLY TWENTIETH CENTURIES

The 1870 Elementary Education Act paved the way for a national system of state schooling, but provision and attendance regulations were not uniform for many decades. Even so, following the act more and more children of both sexes and of all social classes began to attend school for at least a few years. Working- and middle-class girls were being prepared for different lives, and therefore their schooling developed along different lines. We will consider each separately.

SCHOOLS FOR MIDDLE-CLASS GIRLS

The vast majority of schools for middle-class girls were fee-paying establishments. They varied enormously in terms of their aims, curricula and size, and of the clientele they attracted. Some could best be described as domestic boarding establishments, where a small number of girls and young women lived *en famille* and were taught

37

to be 'young ladies' – and very little else. There was an emphasis on learning 'useless' feminine accomplishments. Only subjects which were seen as 'ladylike', such as music, art, fancy needlework, European languages and botany, were taught.

Molly Hughes, who was a pupil at such a school, later commented critically on her experience:

> In my twelfth year my mother decided to send me to an 'Establishment for Young Ladies' about a mile from home. It must have been to give me some companionship, for I can conceive no other rational motive for the step. Indeed, I have come to think that the main value of school life is to prevent one's getting on too fast in the natural surroundings of home. (M. Hughes, 1934)

Schools like this were common and it is estimated that, in 1889, 70 per cent of middle-class girls over the age of 11 who went to school attended them (Marks, 1976).

Academic education for girls was highly controversial and the founders of schools which offered a curriculum coming close to, if not actually comparable to, that offered to boys faced considerable opposition and prejudice. Their task was not easy. They required 'an unusual combination of qualities, for they had to work out their own methods, and form their own traditions, and to do this without alienating timid parents still fearful of too much change' (Sturge, 1932). A major reason why parents were apprehensive was the existence of a considerable body of opinion which held that studying subjects such as mathematics and science was actually injurious to girls' health and likely to threaten their femininity and their reproductive potential. Even if they managed to achieve motherhood, some authorities warned that

> in its full sense, the reproductive power means the power to bear a well-developed infant, and to supply that infant with the natural food for the natural period. Most of the flat-chested girls who survive their high-pressure education are incompetent to do this. (H. Spencer, 1867)

Too much education was felt to be too physically wearing, and formal schooling beyond puberty was often not encouraged. Indeed, as late as 1908 it was being argued that after girls reached the age of 13 or 14,

> as regards mental work, great care should be taken to avoid any undue strain. Lessons requiring much concentration, and therefore using up a great deal of brain energy, Mathematics, for instance, should not be pushed. With some girls it is well to discontinue one or more subjects for a time if they begin to show signs of fatigue . . . Such subjects as cookery, embroidery or the handicrafts may well be introduced into the curriculum as they cause comparatively little mental strain. (Campbell, 1908)

Consequently quite a lot of day schools for middle-class girls only had morning sessions, with the afternoons being available for girls to learn their female duties from their mothers.

Sara Delamont has usefully categorized the pioneering reformers of girls' and womens' education into 'separatists' and 'uncompromisers' (Delamont, 1978). 'Separatists', like Dorothea Beale of Cheltenham Ladies College, wanted higher standards of education for women and girls, but did not demand the same treatment or access to the same curricula as men and boys. 'Uncompromisers', on the other hand, were convinced that the only way to achieve equality was to insist that girls and women study the same subjects, sit the same examinations and be judged by the same standards as boys and men. The schools which were started by 'non-compromisers', including those set up by the Girls' Public Day Schools Trust and the North London Collegiate School founded by Frances Buss, tended to be modelled on boys' public schools, with an emphasis on sport and competition.

Both 'separatists' and 'non-compromisers' aimed to turn out middle-class women and both, therefore, faced a fundamental dilemma caused by conflict between, on the one hand, conventions of femininity and what were regarded as appropriate activities and behaviour for middle-class females and, on the other hand, the male academic establishment. In other words, if 'educated women' wanted to retain their femininity and be seen to act and behave in the way appropriate for 'proper' women, then behaviours, standards and values associated with the 'educated man' were out of the question. Adopting 'male' characteristics and traits meant rejecting 'female' ones, and society was very hard on those who did what was seen as being such an unnatural thing. For this reason 'uncompromisers' faced much greater resistance than 'separatists'.

There was no real solution to the dilemma. 'Uncompromisers' aimed to prove that educated women and girls could still be feminine by insisting on respectable womanly dress, deportment and behaviour. 'Separatists' did the same, and also emphasized that certain subjects were more suitable for females. Their strategies to gain acceptance in the late nineteenth and early twentieth centuries continue to have repercussions for schooling today, particularly with regard to what is deemed to be 'appropriate' in terms of dress, sports and subjects for boys and girls.

Regardless of whether they attended a school dominated by 'separatists' or 'uncompromisers', most girls had to decide between studying and a 'career' on the one hand, and marriage and a family on the other. The two were seen as incompatible, even by some 'uncompromising' teachers themselves. Elizabeth Garrett Anderson, who was a famous doctor as well as a wife and mother, was a notable exception, but on the whole it was seen as rather degrading for middle-class women to undertake paid work, and even some who advocated education for women did so on the grounds that it would make them better companions for their husbands.

There were girls' schools which did encourage girls to think in terms of a career and thereby of economic independence. Frequently, however, work was presented as an alternative to marriage, and the role model of the spinster teacher, which provided many girls with their only experience of (middle-class) working women, tended to be viewed as not very appealing. The headmistress of Manchester High School herself accepted that this was a problem when she suggested that:

> A girl's teacher is, in general, a student and a spinster – not a woman leading the normal ordinary woman's life; a woman who too often is not living in a home at all, even as a sister or daughter. This tends to distort the girl's ideas, and makes her think that she, too would be a teacher, and live this abnormal life. (Burstall, 1914)

Following the tradition of earlier centuries, certain Catholic orders founded academic schools for girls. In these schools there was a tension between the emphasis on the pursuit of academic excellence and the requirements of ideal Catholic womanhood as mother or nun. Nevertheless, even after the carnage wrought by the First World War forced more women into supporting themselves, marriage continued to be the goal of the majority.

It should also be pointed out that it is not strictly accurate to say that girls had to decide on what they wanted from their lives, because for many there was no real choice. Their families simply would not have countenanced spending money on further study and would also have regarded it as deviant and unnatural that their daughters should even want to pursue such a route. Indeed, up until the time of the First World War (and no doubt beyond) there was a strong feeling in many circles that schooling encouraged the wrong kind of aspirations in girls, and undermined their attachment to home and appreciation of domestic duties. Vera Brittain, for example, recorded in her autobiography how her pursuit of higher education was regarded by her family and her peers:

> though my budding ambition to go to college . . . met with real sympathy from both Principals and staff [at school], it received no practical preparation for the necessary exams . . . No doubt my father's persistent determination throughout my schooldays that I should be turned into an entirely ornamental young lady deterred [the school Principals] from the efforts they would otherwise have made on my behalf . . . My classroom contemporaries regarded my ambitions, not unnaturally, with no particular interest or sympathy. Many of them were fashionable young women to whom universities represented a quite unnecessary prolongation of useless and distasteful subjects . . . Both for [them] and their mothers, the potential occurrence that loomed largest upon the horizon was marriage. (Brittain, 1933)

STATE SCHOOLS FOR WORKING-CLASS GIRLS

In the state sector the push for universal state schooling came from a number of sources. Chief among these were the following:

1 The influence of reformers who believed in the notion of 'childhood'. They held that children were, and should be, treated differently from adults and that full-time work for children was inappropriate and injurious to their development.
2 The strong current of opinion connected with the growing demands for universal suffrage and democratic forms of government. In this view, a higher standard of public education would serve as the mark of an advanced and humanitarian civilization and would be generally beneficial for individuals and the nation as a whole.
3 The eugenic argument, based on fears about the quality and quantity of the population. These fears were fuelled at the time of the Boer War when large numbers of working-class volunteers failed the medicals. As far as women were concerned this was a deficit argument, because they were seen as to blame for the general poor state of health. It was claimed that they were ignorant about basic hygiene, nutrition and child-care and that, therefore, if there was to be any improvement, remedial action was necessary. Schools were seen as the places to provide it. Of course, the eugenic argument took little or no account of the conditions in which many working-class families had to live – conditions which made health and adequate diets and standards of hygiene difficult, if not impossible, to achieve.
4 Particularly at the end of the nineteenth and the beginning of the twentieth centuries, the strong moves for schools to take a much more active and central role in training working-class girls for domestic service. These girls, in contrast to those from the middle classes, were not seen to be in any danger from onerous work.
5 The role an educated workforce could play in the development of the economy.

The curriculum for working-class girls in state elementary schools placed the emphasis on domestic skills. Girls spent long periods of time sewing, knitting and laundering, often practising on garments belonging to teachers or, particularly in rural areas, members of the 'gentry'. When facilities were available they learnt 'plain' cookery. Child-care also began to be taught. Ironically, many girls were frequently kept at home to do just the things they were supposed to be learning about at school. When, albeit rarely, science was included in the curriculum it was often linked to domesticity by, for instance, focusing on the properties of cleansing agents.

When attendance at school did become the norm boys and girls were differentiated from their first day. Although around half of all elementary schools were co-educational, the sexes were often segregated for some if not all classes, and there were usually separate playgrounds.

Following the 'Free Places in Secondary Schools: Supplementary Regulation' in 1907 there was an increase in the number of scholarship places to grammar schools. This never had a great effect on the opportunities of working-class children, particularly girls. Even those who won places were often unable to take them up because their parents could not afford the loss of a wage, or to buy the required uniform and other necessities. If a girl passed the examination, a grammar school education was often seen as a waste of time because she was expected to get married anyway. Those few working-class children who did go to grammar schools frequently found it difficult to cope because they lacked the social knowledge and skills necessary for success. The greater number of scholarships did have some effect on the experiences of some middle-class girls, but even so boys reaped the main benefit.

Grammar schools tended to follow the 'public school' model with a 'masculine' emphasis. Many were single-sex, and many of those for girls did place a high premium on study and on going to university, or to teacher training college as a second best (although marriage was still regarded as highly important). Even then, it was not easy for girls to gain access to higher education, and if they got to university they were in the minority and not always that well accepted. For women who had been to university and gained a degree the career choices were not extensive, with teaching generally being regarded as the most 'acceptable', if not the only, work for women.

LEGISLATION, MAJOR EDUCATION ACTS, REPORTS AND INNOVATIONS

After the First World War, education came to be seen as a basic right which it was the duty of the state to provide, particularly if parents were not in a position to pay for it themselves. Consequently, education became a major area of parliamentary and party political concern and has since been the subject of various major acts and reports. In the remainder of this chapter we will be looking at what some of these acts and reports have meant for girls' schooling in the state sector, in so far as they have implied preparation for future life.

The Hadow Report of 1926 had considerable influence on the education of older working-class girls and boys (that is, those aged 11 and over). It paved the way for the tripartite system of grammar, modern and technical schools by proposing the establishment of 'modern' schools for those – the majority – who were not selected for, or were unable to take up places at, grammar or technical schools. In modern schools the bias was towards 'practical work and realistic studies' in preparation for adult life, with the expected stereotypical differences for boys and girls. For example, housecraft was necessary in order to 'render girls fit on leaving school to undertake intelligently the various household duties which devolve on most women' (Board of Education, 1926, p. 232). Paid employment for girls was mentioned, but only in the restricted 'feminine' areas of dressmaking, millinery, artistic embroidery and needlecraft.

Reorganization of schools along the lines suggested by Hadow began in the 1930s and was formalized by the 1944 Education Act. This act was extremely important in that it put the responsibility for schooling the majority of the population firmly in the hands of the state, to be administered by the LEAs. The act reorganized schooling into three stages, primary, secondary and further education, and raised the leaving age to 15 (this part of the act came into operation in 1947). The welfare obligations and powers of LEAs were increased with regard to such things as providing school meals, medicals, clothing grants, transport and scholarships. The act attempted to address educational inequality based on social class by making access to grammar schools dependent on merit and on passing an examination. (That it failed to do so is another story.) It did not, however, question traditional differences in the nature of girls' and boys' education. The belief that such differences were 'natural' and necessary was deep-rooted. Writing in 1948, John Newsom, an influential schools inspector, was voicing public opinion and 'common sense' when he stated that:

> Women possess certain particular needs based on their particular psychology, physiology and their social and economic position . . . The fundamental common experience is the fact that the vast majority of them will become the makers of homes, and that to do this successfully requires the proper development of many talents. (Newsom, 1948, p. 110)

By the time of the 1959 Crowther Report on the education of 15- to 18-year-olds, the situation had not changed with regard to differential expectations for girls and boys. The report talked about the wastage of female ability due to the fact that girls left school earlier than boys, even though more secondary modern school girls than boys said they would have liked to stay on longer. Early leaving prevented girls getting higher and professional qualifications. Despite lamenting this wastage, Crowther noted that the 'needs' of 'less able' – that is, working-class – girls

> are much more sharply differentiated from those of boys of the same age than is true of the academically abler group. Nearly nine times as many girls as boys get married before they are 19. This is reflected in the immediate interests of the boys and girls in the last year or two of the school course. There can be no doubt that at this stage boys' thoughts turn most often to a career, and only secondly to marriage and the family; and that the converse obtains with girls. It is plain then, that, if it is sound

educational policy to take account of natural interests, there is a clear case for a curriculum which respects the different roles they play. (CACE, 1959, para. 51)

So, boys were to have careers while women had families. Yet certain careers were suggested as being particularly suitable to be combined with marriage. Not surprisingly these were in the fields of teaching, social work, health services, the clothing trades and commerce (para. 49).

In 1962 there was the Newsom Report, *Half Our Future*, on the secondary education of students of 'less than average ability' (allegedly half the population and predominantly the working class). This too was based on the sorts of assumption about boys' and girls' differential interests and destinations that informed the Crowther Report. For example: 'For all girls . . ., there is a group of interests relating to what many, perhaps most of them, would regard as their most important vocational concern, marriage' (CACE, 1962, para. 113).

So far, the reports we have referred to have all been concerned with secondary education. Preparation for life is clearly likely to be a significant curricular influence during the last few years of school. It is also important in the primary years too (as we shall see in Chapter 4). The influential Plowden Report of 1967 focused on primary education, and although ostensibly eschewing differentiation between boys and girls, it still assumed traditional sex roles. For instance, a photograph in the report captioned 'Looking forward to adult life' (CACE, 1967, Plate 9) shows two girls and one boy. The girls, one of whom wears a nurse's cap, are bathing a baby doll, while the boy has a stethoscope and is, presumably, the doctor.

At the time when they were written, these reports reflected public opinion regarding differentiation between girls and boys. As we have already noted, such differences were regarded as 'natural' and innate and were accorded little or no significance by most educationalists, sociologists or psychologists. Social class continued to be the major focus of concern, and worries about the differential achievement of working- and middle-class pupils contributed to the introduction of comprehensive schools. The movement towards comprehensive education gained impetus following the issue by a Labour government in 1965 of 'Circular 10/65: The Organization of Secondary Education'. This required LEAs to submit plans for school reorganization which would eliminate selection at 11. One consequence was a dramatic decrease in the number of single-sex schools. This had implications for students and teachers and there is now a body of evidence which has prompted a reconsideration of the social and academic benefits and problems for girls and women of co-education (see Deem, 1984, and Chapter 8 in this book for further discussion).

The 1960s and 1970s saw many changes in social values and attitudes. It was during this time that the issues raised by the 'Women's

Liberation Movement' began to gain wide public recognition. Gender became problematic and more people began to think more about and to question what they had hitherto taken for granted. Putting gender on the agenda led to the passing, in 1975, of the Sex Discrimination Act. The act made it illegal to deny access to goods, facilities, services, premises, education or employment on the grounds of sex. Ironically, in the same year, a Department of Education and Science (DES) survey on 'Curricular differences for boys and girls' was also published. This revealed that boys and girls were prepared for different roles in life and encouraged to accept these gender differences as normal. Boys and girls were offered different subject options. When, in 1975, this became illegal, schools often successfully argued against change and prosecution on the grounds that they lacked sufficient facilities.

Overall the Sex Discrimination Act has proved to be difficult to enforce generally, and in schools in particular, because it is often hard to 'prove' sex discrimination. For those who have pursued cases, the personal costs have usually been great and this has tended to be a deterrent. Indeed, the act has signally failed to challenge structural inequalities and this task has been largely left to individuals and pressure groups. It was these individuals and groups who, throughout the 1970s and 1980s, launched a variety of national, local and school-based gender initiatives and projects.

Among the most well known projects are 'Girls Into Science and Technology' (GIST) and 'Girls And Technology Education' (GATE). These have tried to encourage girls in areas which have traditionally been perceived as 'male territory'. They provided such resources as project teams with experience and expertise who worked alongside teachers, and in-service opportunities. But they could only have any success ('success' in terms of girls taking more positive views of science) if the schools in which they were implemented had conducive, thoroughly supportive climates. Such support was relatively rare and 'success' was limited. Furthermore, teachers were reluctant to acknowledge any changes in their practice as a result of being involved in the project (see Kelly, Whyte and Smart, 1984; Whyte, 1985).

Over the years there have been other projects such as the Schools' Council Sex Differentiation Project (see Millman and Weiner, 1985) and Genderwatch (see Myers, 1987), which have looked at sex and gender differentiation in schools and, particularly in the case of 'Genderwatch', have offered strategies for tackling it. (In 1989, however, because of its widespread use in schools, Genderwatch was out of print and reprinting had to be privately financed. This represents the level of official support received by many equal opportunities ventures).

Some Certificate of Pre-Vocational Education (CPVE) and other pre-vocational courses, for students over the compulsory leaving age, had taken the promotion of equal opportunities as an aim and begun to consider ways of breaking down rigid sex-stereotyped choice in vocational courses, but these had only touched a few students. Then, in 1983, came TVEI. The Technical and Vocational Education Initiative, funded by the Manpower Services Commission (MSC, which later became the Training Agency), firmly placed equal opportunities – gender – on the educational agenda and forced LEAs and schools at least to consider and pay lip-service to the issues and implications of entitlement (see below).

The aim of TVEI was to 'improve' and 'develop' the existing provision in technical and vocational education for 14- to 18-year-olds, because it was felt to be inadequate and the cause of the country's poor showing in the international market (a deficit argument). In order to qualify for special TVEI funding – which, in the days before all secondary schools came to be involved, was very generous – certain criteria had to be met. One criterion concerned equal opportunities and stated that:

> Each project should comprise one or more sets of full time programmes with the following characteristics: equal opportunities should be available to young people of both sexes and they should be educated together on courses within each project. Care should be taken to avoid sex stereotyping. (MSC, 1984)

Despite this requirement the courses provided under TVEI tended to be sex-stereotyped and students tended to opt for 'traditional' subjects. Indeed, the vocational nature of the schemes possibly caused a higher degree of sex-segregation in schools because of the division of labour in society and the different status attached to 'female' and 'male' jobs. Although the MSC were aware of this they did not actually withdraw funds for failing to meet the criterion. Even so, TVEI did make some schools and colleges more aware of their responsibility to address gender inequalities in a broader sense than just attracting students into non-traditional courses. It also funded seminars and conferences at which people could share ideas and explore strategies for improving the situation. In addition, a number of LEAs used part of their TVEI budgets to pay for equal opportunities posts and in-service education, and in some places these were incorporated into general LEA provision.

We will now move on to what has been described as 'the beginning of a new era' (Kenneth Baker, *The Times*, 30 July 1988). This dawned in 1988 when a Conservative government passed the Education Reform Act (ERA). This was the most important piece of educational legislation since 1944 and it has had considerable effects on and implications for schools and schooling. In general, ERA represented increased central control over education and the limitation of the power and authority of LEAs. More control was given to school governors, and individual state schools were granted more power over their own finances. A National Curriculum for 5- to 16-year-olds, together with requirements for pupils to be assessed at 7, 11 and 14, was also introduced.

The National Curriculum is based on the concept of 'entitlement', which involves the provision of 'balanced and broad' schooling for all, aimed at widening students' range of experiences and encouraging informed choices and increasing expectations. A core curriculum followed by all students in state schools, regardless of their sex, 'race', class, ability or what school they attend, does theoretically have some potential for enhancing equality of opportunity, especially in secondary schools where students are able to opt for particular subjects. It is not, however, that simple, even though the guide to the implementation of the National Curriculum stresses that 'The *whole* curriculum for *all* pupils will certainly need to include at appropriate (and in some cases all) stages: . . . coverage across the curriculum of gender and multi-cultural issues' (DES, 1989c, para. 3.8).

CONCLUSION

Throughout the history of schools and schooling it has been taken for granted that boys and girls are different, and the reasons for these 'differences' have generally been seen as relatively unimportant. By and large, however, they have tended to be seen as 'natural' rather than social and cultural. This is convenient because it means there can be no remedy. Official attempts to 'improve' women's access to schooling and education have generally been economically motivated and aimed at improving the workforce rather than improving women's lives.

The past has created a legacy for the present for both boys and girls. This is not, however, to say that things cannot change. They clearly can and indeed have changed. For example, when the authors of this book were at school during the 1950s, 1960s and 1970s it was almost unheard of for boys to take needlework and girls woodwork, and if anyone challenged the reasons for this they were regarded as deviant for questioning the 'natural' and 'normal' order of things. Now co-educational craft groups are quite common, at least in the early years. Yet there is a long way to go, and in subsequent chapters we will be looking at why this might be and areas where change is still needed.

CHAPTER SUMMARY

This chapter has looked briefly at the recent history of schooling for girls. Expectations about girls' future life and the role of women has

meant that the curriculum for both middle- and working-class girls has focused mainly on domestic subjects and 'feminine accomplishments'. Those who have campaigned for a more academic education have met with strong resistance and have had to take steps to prove that educated women could still be feminine.

The assumption that women will marry, look after homes and raise children has been reflected in many major reports on and recommendations for education, and until the late 1960s gender differentiation in schools was not regarded as an issue. Concern about inequality centred on the relative achievements of working- and middle-class pupils, and even then boys were the main focus.

In 1975 the passing of the Sex Discrimination Act made it illegal to deny access to education on the basis of sex. However, cases have been hard to prove and the act has failed to challenge structural inequality. Similarly a National Curriculum followed by all pupils, as introduced under the 1988 Education Reform Act, does little to combat structural sexism because it does not inevitably change male-dominated forms of organization, or attitudes, expectations or stereotypes.

KEY DATES

1850 North London Collegiate School founded

1853 Cheltenham Ladies College founded

1870 Elementary Education Act paved the way for a national system of state schooling

1874 Girton (women's) College, Cambridge, founded

1878 University of London admitted women to full degrees

1879 Lady Margaret Hall and Somerville (women's) Colleges, Oxford, founded

1907 Free Places in Secondary Schools: Supplementary Regulation increased the number of scholarships to grammar schools

1920 Oxford University admitted women to full degrees

1926 Hadow Report proposed a tripartite system with 'practical work and realistic studies' in preparation for adult life in modern schools

1944 Education Act, aimed largely at addressing inequality based on social class, implemented tripartite system

1947 Cambridge University admitted women to full degrees

1959 Crowther Report referred to wastage of female talent due to girls leaving school early

1963 Newsom Report assumed working-class girls' most important concern was marriage

1965 'Circular 10/65: The Organization of Secondary Education' reduced the number of single-sex schools

1967   Plowden Report draws attention to importance of primary education in the preparation for life

1975   Sex Discrimination Act

1975   DES survey 'Curricular differences for boys and girls', revealed differential schooling

1983   TVEI

1988   Education Reform Act requires common experience

SUGGESTIONS FOR FURTHER READING

Delamont, S. (1989) *Knowledgeable Women: Structuralism and the Reproduction of Elites*. London: Routledge. This very readable book focuses on the education and professional training of clever middle- and upper-class women.

Dyhouse, C. (1981) *Girls Growing up in Late Victorian and Edwardian England*. London: Routledge & Kegan Paul. This book considers the socialization and education of girls at home within the family and in the wider social context.

Hunt, F. (ed.) (1987) *Lessons for Life: The Schooling of Girls and Women 1850–1950*. Oxford: Basil Blackwell. This collection of papers on historical aspects of female schooling is divided into three sections: ideologies in education, inequalities in education, and experiences in education.

Purvis, J. (1991) *A History of Women's Education in England*. Milton Keynes: Open University Press. This book concentrates on the education of working- and middle-class girls and women in the years between 1800 and 1914. It makes much use of the writings and talk of women and girls themselves to show how, although education could be a liberating experience, it was extremely difficult to escape from the expected domestic role.

CHAPTER 4

The early years: nursery and primary school

CHAPTER OVERVIEW

In this chapter we look at gender in the early years of a child's life. There is no fully worked out understanding of the processes involved in gender construction, but researchers have developed a number of suggestions about the socialization involved. We will look at work done on the family, playgroups and nursery and primary schools. How does gender identity contribute to the child's experience of and success in school? Are there differences in boys' and girls' experiences of school, and does this have an effect on how well they do there?

This chapter looks at gender in a child's early years. It is clear of course that the early experiences in a child's life can be vital in determining her/his later attitudes and expectations, and feminists argue that this is as true for gender as for other areas.

Sex role socialization begins in the family, and nursery and primary schools continue the process and play a part in constructing gender through their organization and practices. They 'fix' gender identities. Feminists argue that gender socialization lays down attitudes and even aptitudes and skills that affect achievement levels throughout the pupil's career.

There are two main issues in this chapter. The first is gender socialization – the processes that construct the gender of the child. The second is the way that the child's experience of gender socialization affects her/his responses to and experience of school and ultimately her/his success or failure there.

FAMILY AND THE PRE-SCHOOL PHASE

We have already said in Chapter 1 that all the processes involved in constructing gender are not fully understood and that there are a number of different and competing theoretical approaches. Feminist research over the last ten or fifteen years has drawn our attention to the fact that girls and boys are treated differently from birth. In most maternity hospitals sex-typed comments on the behaviour and appearance of newborn babies are common. 'Girl babies are told they are pretty, and some hospitals keep different coloured blankets for girl and boy babies' (Oakley, 1972, p. 173). Indeed, it was the experience of both authors of this book when they had babies that the hospital kept pink blankets for girl and blue blankets for boy babies. Feminists have suggested that these responses from the social world mark the beginning of a gender learning process which is critically important for the child.

The different treatment continues through childhood. Spender (1979) identifies some of the ways this happens, shown here in the boxed text.

Names

Boys are given names which are short and 'hard hitting' while girls are given fussy and pert names.

Toys

Boys are bought adventure, action, 'doing' toys; girls' toys involve nurture, cleaning and grooming. A glance at television advertising of children's toys makes this clear.

Clothing

Boys are bought clothes which are easy to move and play in, and allow them freedom. Girls are still bought clothes which do not encourage activity and freedom of movement.

The street

In the family, sex-differentiated treatment in terms of physical contact, verbal communication, dress and toys succeeds in forming firm gender identities. Segregation begins in the family, where there is likely to be a sharply defined sexual division of labour. It is reinforced in the 'street'.

> ### *Play*
>
> Hart (1979) showed that boys are allowed more physical freedom than girls and are not kept so close to home. It is important to note that social class may have an influence here (Newson, 1976). As the child, becomes 'increasingly acquainted with the outside world, via contact with other children, television, comics and story books, what they have learned about sex-appropriate behaviour is reinforced' (Spender and Sarah, 1980).

We have already suggested in Chapter 1 that explanations like this, which stress social learning, may tell only part of the story about the way gender is constructed. Their advantage is that they indicate very clearly the differences in the ways we treat children and segregate them.

However, this approach has been criticized for being too deterministic. It sees society as crudely imposing sex role stereotypes upon the individual. We need to remember that children also socialize each other. We suggested earlier that cognitive development theories, which see the child as more self-socializing and active in formulating sex role concepts, are important too. It is probable that imitation, modelling, reinforcement and cognitive processes all play a part in children's sex role socialization. There is some research work which aims to look at what goes on in families and schools in the light of this theory. However, we need more new research which takes the more complex theoretical approaches and looks at them in detail in the early years of a child's life.

What is clear is that by the time children come to school, they have already acquired a set of attitudes and expectations about what girls and boys can and should do. There is no suggestion that schools alone are responsible for the process, nor that schools in any way contravene the general thinking of society.

PLAYGROUP, NURSERY SCHOOL AND PRIMARY SCHOOL

The second major institution after the family to play a role in the lives of many children in Britain is the playgroup or nursery school, followed by the primary school. We have chosen to look at nursery and primary school in the same section because so many of the issues are the same. There is a widely held belief that in nurseries boys and girls are given greater equality of treatment than in later stages of schooling, but recent work contradicts this (Browne and France, 1986; Hodgeon, 1988).

Gender and achievement in the early years

The large-scale studies of children's achievement that have been done show that girls consistently do better than boys academically through their primary education in all subjects, with the possible exception of mathematics (Douglas, 1964; Davie *et al.*, 1972). This situation changes when girls reach secondary school, and girls begin to fail. We will look in the next chapter at some of the factors that research has suggested are responsible for causing this underachievement in secondary school. However, this does not mean that we can ignore what goes on in primary schools, as there is evidence that some later problems stem from the primary phase of schooling.

Boys and girls underachieve in specific areas of the curriculum: as a general rule girls tend to do well at language-based skills and boys do better on the mathematical and scientific side of the curriculum. We know that boys seem to have more difficulty learning to read than girls, and we know that girls have more problems with mathematics. However, there is substantial controversy now over the issue of girls' performance in maths (Isaacson, 1988, gives a full review). The main issue is the age at which girls' performance in mathematics begins to fade in comparison with boys. One group of researchers is convinced that 'the main differences in performance are already established by age 11' (Joffe and Foxman, 1984). The other group is convinced that the problems do not start until after the age of 11 and the question is really one for secondary age children. We will introduce the issue in this chapter on primary school.

SCHOOLS AND SEX ROLE SOCIALIZATION

In this chapter we need to look at what feminist writers have to say about the ways that schools contribute to and affect these problems. The following list gives suggestions about what is important:

1 The organization of the school.
2 The organization and management of classrooms and lessons.
3 The curriculum.
4 Children's experience of the curriculum.
5 Teachers' activities and actions.
6 The hidden curriculum.

7   Teachers' career structures.
8   Children's informal culture.

ORGANIZATION OF THE SCHOOL

Pupils in primary schools are frequently divided into single-sex groups for activities where gender is irrelevant. Official record cards in schools may be colour-coded differently for boys and for girls. There may be separate listings of boys' and girls' names on the register, with boys' names being called first, although there is no reason why there cannot be simple alphabetical order. Boys and girls in many primary schools have separate places to hang up their coats, and toilet facilities are frequently segregated. Girls and boys may even have separate lines in the playground, and outside classrooms. King (1978) describes this, and gives an account of the kinds of joke that it leads to, which give children gender messages. For example, one day a teacher ridiculed a child by commenting, 'Oh, Philip is a little girl. He's in the wrong queue.' One implication of this segregated organization is that children are called to do out-of-lesson activities in single-sex groups; for example, they sit apart in assembly and perhaps for lunch. It may encourage children to assume that they should operate in single-sex groups.

Primary schools cannot enforce regulations on uniforms, but dress codes too may be different. In some schools girls and even their teachers are not allowed to wear trousers, or shorts in the summer. Holly (1985) gives an account of the way that one head, who said he was committed to equal opportunities for boys and girls, tried to forbid the girls wearing shorts one summer. 'Fortunately he was defeated by the fact that so many girls continued to come to school in shorts despite his demand that they "dress like girls"' (p. 53).

In Flag Junior School, where one of the authors, Lynda Measor, did some research, the head developed an interesting strategy. (The school is a large junior school in a suburban area of the southeast of England. It is largely but by no means exclusively middle-class.) The uniform for winter was a tartan skirt for girls and grey trousers for boys. Girls were officially allowed to wear trousers, but they had to be tartan ones, which were difficult to find, so the girls all wore skirts.

ORGANIZATION AND MANAGEMENT OF CLASSROOMS AND LESSONS

Feminist research has presented evidence to suggest that teachers frequently organize and manage their classrooms and lessons on the basis of gender. Teachers very often use the strategy of competition between boys and girls to motivate both to work harder. There are many examples: King quotes one teacher who said, 'Boys close eyes. Girls creep out quietly. Don't let the boys hear you' (King, 1978, p. 49). In a game of general knowledge girls and boys were constantly pitted against each other. If the boys won there was a loud, triumphant roar (Clarricoates, 1980, p. 30). Teachers frequently organize races between boys and girls to see who can finish off their work first.

At Flag School Lynda recorded another example. At the end of the school day, the teacher organized a competition between the different tables to see which was ready first and so could be the first to leave. The children sat largely in sex-segregated groups. Tables with girls were often ready first and the teacher commended them for this, for being tidy, for sitting up straight and for being quiet, and allowed them to go first.

What are the implications of these practices? Do they matter? Sociobiologists, for example, would want to question why this is a problem. They maintain that schools are only doing what is 'natural', in distinguishing between natural differences and making normal boys and girls. Feminist researchers, however, have suggested that these practices are important because they frequently remind pupils that they are either male or female (Delamont, 1990). Researchers suggest such activities are significant in the process of 'fixing' gender identity and have a long-term effect in limiting opportunity and life chances.

THE CURRICULUM

Feminist research has drawn our attention to the fact that some schools have offered a sex-segregated curriculum. The Sex Discrimination Act (1975) created some guidelines, but girls and boys were still doing different things in school. Until the development of the National Curriculum it was possible for boys and girls to be offered and taught quite different subjects in school. One of the things that feminist research over the last ten years has argued most effectively is that equal access to the same curriculum is essential (EOC, 1987). The National Curriculum has the potential to bring large-scale change in this area.

In most primary schools, the curriculum is largely the same for both sexes. It is usually only the craft and games areas in which children are offered different material. In Hayes School, the middle school Lynda Measor studied in 1981, there was what is perhaps a typical pattern: boys were offered woodwork and girls needlework. It is interesting to note that both were offered cookery. However, things are changing. In 1989, Flag School ensured that all children took the full range of subjects, and arranged to have a male teacher for cookery.

In the majority of schools boys and girls are still taught separately for 'games'. In infant schools, they are likely to have PE, games in the hall or moving to music together. In junior or middle school, however, once the children begin to learn sports, the common policy is still to teach games like football or netball in sex-segregated groups:

> TOM The girls used to play last year, but now we learn football skills and they've kind of dropped behind. (Holly, 1989, p. 58).

Flag School adopted a policy to overcome this. Their aim was to teach 'skills', and this was their objective across all curriculum areas, whether language, maths, music or games. The girls did football, because teachers believed they needed the skills of speed and co-ordination as much as the boys.

CHILDREN'S EXPERIENCE OF THE CURRICULUM

The primary school curriculum has always been far less segregated than the secondary, but research has alerted us to the fact that it is not only the issue of the official curriculum that is significant. Children may well be offered much the same things in lessons, but their experience of it may be different.

Curriculum materials and school textbooks

One of the issues that may be important in this context is the kind of material that is contained in school textbooks. It is clear from the research that these can contain strongly sex-stereotyped materials. In the context of primary education, we need also to look at the reading schemes and maths schemes that are used in very many schools – probably the majority of schools. We have fuller research on the reading schemes, and so will look at them first. It is also important to look at the kinds of reading book that are available to children in school.

Reading schemes

Lobban (1975) is perhaps the best-known piece of work on reading schemes. She researched six of the schemes that are used most commonly in British primary schools to teach children to read. Lobban found that the schemes showed women and men doing very different jobs, and leading very different lives. There were more males in the scheme than females (seventy-one males and only thirty-five females). Most of the females were involved in domestic occupations and roles, like looking after a baby. The boys were almost always dominant, with a wider range of things to do, more toys and even more pets. Grown women in the books did not have jobs; their skills were of the domestic, stay-at-home kind.

The significance of these findings is that children spend a considerable time with their reading scheme books, and so the concern is that they are likely to absorb stereotyped roles and expectations about gender at the same time as they learn to read. Children learn that it is 'normal' for mums to stay at home and for dads to go out to work, even if their own experience does not confirm this. (Many reading schemes are biased in terms of social class and 'race' as well as gender.)

Reading books

We do now have detailed studies of the kinds of children's reading book that are on offer (Maccia, Coleman and Estep, 1975; Stacey *et al.*, 1974). The pattern is the same: boys do interesting things, have adventures and lead the girls. Enid Blyton has been especially criticized in this context, and although she is no longer read in many schools we will use her work as an illustration because it shows the problems particularly effectively. In the first 'Secret Seven' book, it is made clear that the boys make the decisions. 'Janet went down to the shed by herself. "Just open the shed and give it an airing" ordered Peter. "We shan't be using it today"' (Blyton, 1989, p. 37). The boys are definitely in charge:

> 'Yes', said Peter. 'Well, let's split up the inquiries. Pam, you go and see if you can find out who owns the house.'
> 'How do we find out?' asked Pam.
> 'You will have to use your common sense', said Peter. 'I can't decide everything. Janet and Barbara, you can go down the lane and examine it for car tracks.' (p. 42)

In traditional fairy stories of course the problem is particularly acute. Princesses wait passively, even asleep in extreme cases, to be rescued by handsome princes on obligatory white horses. The girls involved do not have to do anything for themselves, like study science or get a degree or slog in a factory to make a living; their beauty and their goodness ensure they will be saved. In recent years this has led to a reaction and authors have written quite different stories, with titles like *The Wrestling Princess*, *Princess Polly to the Rescue* and *Lucy and the Big Bad Wolf*. In *Princess Polly*, it is the prince, Tom, who has been captured by Haggis the witch. Princess Polly recognizes Tom's inability to rescue himself; it is clear that she must do it. She gallops away on the finest racehorse, completes three parts of a quest and rescues the prince. *Lucy and the Big Bad Wolf* works on a similar theme. Lucy, on her way to her grandmother's house, meets the wolf on the bus, confronts his wish to eat her, and turns him into a performing dog to rescue the family fortunes. Alternative stories are available. In Chapter 8 we discuss classroom-based work on new approaches to children's stories in detail, and Appendix 1 has suggestions for new literature.

However, as Delamont points out, 'Most British children spend far more time with comics than books, and absorb gender stereotyping from TV, radio and advertising' (Delamont, 1980, p. 19). Braman (1977) and Sharpe (1976) have looked at this material, and argue that it sends a range of sex-stereotyped messages. The suggestion is that teachers should use classroom time to investigate and understand the biases in the media messages. Chapter 8 has details of work that some teachers have done on these themes.

Primary school textbooks

Cairns and Inglis's recent (1989) article on history textbooks in primary schools is one of the few pieces of work that we have on this subject. They aimed to test influential rather than random textbooks, and they looked at the kind of history that is put forward in these books and specifically at the role of women in them. Their conclusions were that political and military history dominates, and other aspects of the past, especially economic, cultural and religious history, are neglected (p. 221).

Overall in all of the textbooks they studied, 21.0 per cent of the content dealt with the history of warfare and only 0.4 per cent of that material concerned the role of women in warfare. Out of all of the material in all of the textbooks only 14.8 per cent dealt with women. It may be argued that there is less material on the role of women because we have only limited knowledge of women in the past, as is certainly true of the Middle Ages, for example. Yet we know more about women's lives in Tudor times or the Victorian age, and the textbooks on these periods show no indication of this. In particular, the economic activities of women are largely ignored; out of ten textbooks, four provided no information on this at all.

Illustrations in the textbooks are similarly biased. The role of women in these books is very largely reduced to fashion. Even Elizabeth I was presented in an oddly passive light in one of the books, in contrast to the robust rule of Henry VIII. In conclusion, it is clear to Cairns and Inglis that 'There seems little doubt that history textbooks for primary school children are still not being written with the provisions of the Sex Discrimination Act of 1975 in mind' (Cairns and Inglis, 1989, p. 226).

We do not to the best of our knowledge have a full-scale analysis of British primary school textbooks in other subject areas for this kind of sex-stereotyped material. Nilson (1973) summarizes the analyses of the American textbooks which have been made and concludes that they provide a similar picture to the reading schemes, with more males and a greater range of roles and occupations for boys.

Maths textbooks

Northam (1982) looked at maths textbooks, and found that here too males and females were portrayed in stereotypical roles. In junior school books men were over-represented, and when girls appeared their roles were strikingly different from the boys'; girls were less likely to be involved in identifying or solving problems, to be skilful and competitive, and to offer to show someone else how to do a maths problem. While girls set standards of behaviour and took accurate records of others' work, they showed little initiative and less inventiveness. Northam concludes that there is a clear tendency to show maths as a male sphere.

It is interesting that the textbook material puts forward a similar picture across all of the curriculum areas. We cannot of course measure the impact of such books, but McDonald (1981), among others, argues that we should not underestimate their impact, especially as they act to reinforce gender stereotypes found elsewhere.

Children's abilities in different curriculum areas

We have already said that boys and girls have differential rates of achievement in primary education, with girls doing better than boys in all subjects except mathematics. In this section we want to look at this issue and at the response that teachers and schools make to it.

Early years' curriculum: 'play' and 'work'

In the nursery and the primary school classroom, researchers have observed that boys and girls choose different kinds of activity and task at times when their choice is free. In American primary schools, Serbin found that boys played with bricks, trucks and climbing apparatus, and girls primarily played at housekeeping tasks (Serbin, 1978). In British nurseries, Hodgeon observed that girls clustered around the 'quiet' activities and often chose domestic-related tasks, while boys chose the outdoor or energetic tasks (Hodgeon, 1988, p. 37). For example:

> 10.00 a.m. Outdoors, fine autumn weather. For twenty minutes a large group of boys climb, shout, run and jump around. The impression is of movement and noise. Meanwhile three girls sit at the side of the play area sharing books with an adult. There is no communication between the two groups. (Hodgeon, p. 64)

The other point the research makes is that children largely played in single-sex groups. At age three there is a considerable degree of friendship and play across the genders, but by four there is much greater development of single-sex play (Hodgeon, 1988, p. 37). Boys and girls choose different activities, and they object to sharing some of them and will actively resist doing so. Boys, for example, take over the outdoor toys and the space reserved for large-scale construction work, and defend them against any female intrusion. It seems that boys 'monopolise and even dominate certain classroom activities, such as constructional toys like Lego, and unless teachers intervene, girls get little opportunity to develop skills in these areas' (Anti-sexist working party, 1985, p. 136).

This picture is perhaps familiar to most teachers, and again it is important to ask whether it matters. We are not surprised, if boys play with cars, trucks and bricks, and we expect little girls to choose dolls and the wendy house. Feminists have suggested, however, that this division of interest and activity is important, because research evidence indicates that all children need a wide range of concrete play experiences, which are essential for later success in learning in a wide range of academic subjects.

School 'work' and school subjects

As they progress through primary education children continue to develop and display differences in the activities they prefer and in their aptitudes for them, which begin to affect their work on school subjects. We have known for some time that boys have greater difficulty in learning to read than girls (St John, 1932; Blom, 1971; Asher and Gottman, 1973). Between 60 and 90 per cent of the children referred for remedial help are boys (Lee, 1980, p. 122). It is also clear that girls have greater difficulty in mathematics, at least in the later years of primary schooling (Weiner, 1980; R. Walden and Walkerdine, 1982; APU, 1982).

Possible explanations

There are a number of competing explanations for this situation, which are linked to the varying theories of socialization and different feminist theories that we described in Chapters 1 and 2. Those who accept biologically determinist explanations point to different inherent abilities as the cause of the imbalance: girls are 'naturally' better at language-based tasks and boys 'naturally' succeed with numbers and logic. Feminist thinking, however, has emphasized motivational factors, which come in part from socialization patterns.

One factor may be the kinds of toy and activity that children choose and are given in their early years. We know that boys are encouraged to play with activity and constructional toys (Arnot, 1986; Delamont, 1989, 1990). The suggestion is that early experience of playing with these kinds of toy can facilitate the developments of mathematical and certain mechanical and spatial skills, which are an important element in the development of later mathematical and scientific skills (Whyte, 1985; Murphy, 1989). While boys are developing their mechanical and spatial skills, they may, however, reduce their chances to learn pre-reading skills. The suggestion is that girls by contrast spend time on activities which facilitate these. Lee (1980) suggests that there is a general expectation among parents and teachers that girls will more naturally like and choose book- and picture-based activities than boys when they are young. Therefore girls are given books and encouraged to spend time in these activities.

Research into gender differences has related the different patterns of nurturing that many boys and girls receive to the different values and views of relevance they develop (Chodorow, 1978; Harding, 1983). This means in the views of some writers that children come to school with a 'learning style' and a sense of which activities are and which are not appropriate for them. The suggestion is that boys tend to view reading as an activity more appropriate for girls than for boys. Kagen (1964), Stein and Smithells (1969), and Neale, Gill and Tismer (1970) have demonstrated that boys tend to have more negative attitudes towards reading than girls do. Girls on the other hand see mathematics as something boys are more likely to find easy than they do (Sutherland, 1983).

We also know something about the importance of self-constructs here. Spencer (M. Spencer, 1976) has commented on the crucial role played by self-constructs in learning and has suggested that the way students view themselves in a learning situation is extremely important. What matters is whether students see themselves as competent and think they are likely to meet with success, because their view of themselves will affect the way they set about trying to complete the task. This notion of self-construct is important in the area of sex-stereotyping. If a child sees a particular activity or skill as the preserve of one sex rather than the other, then s/he may feel tentative about approaching it. This could be part of the explanation for girls' poor achievement in maths and also for boys' poor achievement in reading.

Research on girls and mathematics suggests that this factor seems to operate here. The evidence is that girls in general give up too easily on maths questions they find difficult; certainly they give up before boys do. We know that girls are more prone to being anxious than boys about maths (Sutherland, 1983). The anxiety and feelings of apprehension seem to affect their mathematical thinking and confidence (p. 312), especially after a certain age.

There is evidence that children respond to the curriculum on the basis of gender, which affects their attitudes to different subject areas and their levels of motivation and confidence. A number of factors affects the way they approach the curriculum, but it is important to look at the way schools and teachers respond to the situation. There is evidence that boys get more remedial help with their academic problems than girls do (Isaacson, 1988). We will look in detail at the evidence for this in the next section.

TEACHERS' ACTIVITIES AND ACTIONS

One of the factors that researchers have identified as important for pupils is the attitudes and expectations of teachers. In this section we will also look at research that suggests that boys are able to gain much more of the teacher's attention and help, and that this affects their achievement levels.

Many research studies have suggested that teachers' assumptions and actions about pupils on the basis of class and 'race' affect their performance and achievement. The now classic Rosenthal and Jacobsen (1968) study, which showed how much experimentally manipulated teacher expectations for pupil progress can affect pupils' intellectual growth, makes it clear that teacher expectations are a force to be reckoned with. Expectations can be shown in many ways: through the subtle application of touch, facial expression, eye contact, vocal tone and gesture teachers convey an array of messages about the pupil's place in the classroom and in life, whether they intend to or not.

Much of the research on expectations has been done in the area of 'race' and class, but feminists argue that the findings apply equally to gender. This is inevitably a difficult and controversial area. Many teachers find it hard to look at their own attitudes, and yet a beginning has been made: 'Teachers themselves often have different expectations of girls' and boys' behaviour and achievement, and these are highly influential, we believe, in upholding the assumed innate differences between the sexes' (Anti-sexist Working Party, 1985, p. 136). It is of course unrealistic to discuss teachers as if they are all the same, part of a homogeneous group sharing a single set of values and attitudes. It is the case that since the early 1970s when this material on gender began to be published many teachers have changed their practices in the light of what they have read. However, there is still substantial resistance to change in many primary schools.

Teachers' expectations of girls

Clarricoates identifies the fact that teachers see girls as being more prepared to conform: 'Oh the girls, naturally you can always rely on them to do their work properly' (1980, p. 29); and more motivated: 'Girls always try to answer the questions first' (p. 29). Clarricoates found that primary school teachers' preference was for rigidly conforming girls who facilitated classroom management, but despite this they liked teaching boys more: 'On the whole you can say that the boys are far more capable of learning, much nicer to teach' (p. 151). It is also important to note that teachers thought boys were brighter and more academically capable. Even though girls had the highest marks right through the primary school that she studied, Clarricoates observed that teachers thought that boys were the brightest: 'Although the girls tend to be good at most things, in the end you find it's going to be a boy who's your most brilliant pupil' (p. 33).

It seems that teachers do have different expectations of boy and girl pupils, and the suggestion is that this affects the pupils' performance. The argument is a controversial one, whether it is applied to pupils from a particular social class, ethnic group or gender. Nevertheless, it is an argument that has a reasonable degree of acceptance within the education field.

Inequality in time and attention from teachers

Expectations, however, are not the only issue. Feminist researchers have pointed out that boys get more attention, more teaching and instruction and also more disciplining than girls: 'Boys dominate the physical space of the classroom and the playground and, from our own experience, dominate the teacher's time too' (Anti-sexist working party, 1985, p. 136). The inequality begins early, in nursery school. Hodgeon observed some significant differences in the ways boys and girls were treated (1988). Language and language development are an important objective in nursery and primary schools, but the language interaction that teachers and helpers have with boys is different in quality and quantity to that with girls.

In a mixed nursery class, boys gained more attention than girls. In the first place their questions were answered more frequently and more quickly. The adults listened hard for boys' answers, and sometimes did not hear girls' answers, even right ones, or chose not to attend to them:

ADULT: (looking at a book with Nicola and David) 'Where's Baby Bunting?'
Nicola points correctly, but adult ignores her. David points incorrectly.
ADULT: No, there's Baby Bunting in the river. (Hodgeon, 1988, p. 17)

Secondly, the teachers in Hodgeon's research elaborated the play of boys more than that of girls. When questions arose out of play, or there was the opportunity to develop a theme, teachers offered more explanation and information to boys than to girls; boys were given longer and more thoughtful replies, girls short, simple answers. The teachers saw elaborating play as an important strategy to develop language, and hence foster cognitive development. Teachers chatted socially to girls more than to boys, but their interactions with boys were more complex and more likely to foster cognitive development (Hodgeon, 1988, pp. 18–25).

It may be that teachers give greater attention to boys to compensate, because they are aware that boys' language development is slower than girls'. There are significant differences in the way the education system responds to discrepancies in achievement. Great efforts are made by individual teachers to help boys' language development, and the school system runs remedial classes for boys who need help with their reading. Yet 'when girls slide down in mathematics, that is generally considered as something "natural" about which no active steps need be taken' (Isaacson, 1988, p. 99). There is now a great deal of research which indicates that this pattern continues throughout primary school. Serbin (1978), for example, found that the boys got eight times as much direct instruction as girls did. There is evidence that this continues through secondary and higher education, too.

Another issue is that teachers seem to plan the curriculum and direct the content of their lessons primarily to suit the interests of the boys (Clarricoates, 1980a). Teachers are extremely sensitive to the fact that boys won't have anything to do with things they consider 'cissy' (Shaw, 1980; Spender and Sarah, 1980; Griffith, 1985). Consequently they plan lessons to appeal to them. Girls are expected to accept this material; the things that are seen to interest them are not placed first.

Researchers suggest that the main reasons for this pattern of interaction is the boys' potential for disruption. From nursery onwards, teachers were clear that boys were more likely to cause a disturbance if they did not receive attention and monitoring, and girls were not seen as likely to do this. It seems that even experienced teachers fear the disruption that bored and disaffected boys can cause in a class. In order to maintain order and good management in the classroom, they felt obliged to concentrate on the boys.

The research does raise important questions about the role of the teacher in relation to gender differentiation and patterns of gender inequality. To what extent should teachers be trying to create change? Feminist groups have asserted that 'Primary schools need to challenge these attitudes rather than, as in the past, condone them' (Anti-sexist working party, 1985: 136). In Chapter 8 of this book we will look in detail at attempts that have been made to try to change the situation.

HIDDEN CURRICULUM

There is one other area of school practices and processes to consider in relation to gender socialization and differentiation. Research in education has drawn our attention to the hidden curriculum, which clearly has an important influence upon what children learn:

The official curriculum details the skills the pupils are supposed to be learning and the avowed aims of the school and the education system of which it is part. A number of authors have shown that the pupil learns a variety of other things in addition to mastering or failing at academic skills . . . The term 'hidden curriculum' is used to describe this learning (Lobban, 1975, p. 52)

Feminist researchers have looked at the influence of the hidden curriculum. They suggest that patterns of interaction, the way children are treated by teachers and by other adults in the school and teachers' classroom management strategies indicate a social code for children's behaviour. Teachers may also act as role models for children, showing this social code for them to follow. We have already discussed how some of these messages are communicated indirectly in the formal organization and curriculum patterns of the school. Here we will look at patterns of interaction between teachers and pupils.

Language

Browne and France (1983) have drawn our attention to the fact that adults do not use the same language with boys and girls at nursery school age, and talk to them very differently. 'Girls were bombarded with terms of endearment, "honey, sweetie, lovey, darling, treasure, precious", whereas boys got terms that reinforce the tough macho behaviour expected of them – "buster, bruiser, toughie, big bully, wise guy" and so on' (p. 150). While they are very young, boys are also offered terms of endearment, but it is not appropriate, it seems, to offer them to older nursery school boys. Browne and France comment, 'Examining the way we talk to young children can be a revealing practice. Young children hear sex stereotyped language, but also they are encouraged to use it' (Browne and France, 1986, p. 147).

Physical appearance

There are other areas in which children are treated differently. Browne and France noted, 'Our obsession with attractive physical appearance in girls crops up in conversations between adults and children in the nursery' (p. 152). Adelman (1979) agrees; he quotes one teacher as follows:

TEACHER: Oh don't you look beautiful. Oh my favourite lady. Do you know, Jane Hopcroft, you look absolutely smashing. (p. 56)

Teachers also discussed girls' clothes: 'Hello Teresa, what a lovely hat. It has got a bobble on the top' (Adelman, p. 93). At no point is any personal comment about appearance addressed to any boys.

Social codes of behaviour

In these ways teachers communicate messages to children about gender and about the ways to be a 'proper' girl or boy. King (1978) identified a code of what counts as appropriate behaviour from boys and girls: girls are told to 'look pretty' and not to 'shout' (p. 54), and expected to set a good example in behaviour, while it is boys who are asked to carry books and chairs, although at primary school age the girls are likely to be bigger and stronger.

It is most often teachers' anecdotal asides which reveal the most stereotyped attitudes toward gender, at the times when teachers are trying their hardest to bring material to life and to be child-centred. King (1978) describes an incident in which the children find a snail in the wet sand box. When a girl went to touch it, the teacher said, 'Ugh, don't touch it, it's all slimy. One of the boys pick it up and put it outside' (p. 43).

Teachers said that they thought boys were more aggressive: 'We have a lot of humdingers in this school; mind you I blame it on the parents' (Clarricoates, 1980, p. 30). Different standards of tolerance were applied, and also the same behaviour was categorized differently depending on the sex. Boys were allowed to be noisier and to get away with more of this aggression, but 'It is not nice to see a young girl fighting' (Clarricoates, p. 32).

Gender codes also seem to vary according to regional and social class. Clarricoates studied four primary schools in very different areas of northern England. Dockside was a traditional working-class school in an urban area and fishing port. Applegate by contrast was set in a modern, suburban, middle-class district, serving mainly settled, prosperous, home-owning, professional parents. Long Estate was a new primary school, built on a new council estate. Linton Bray was set in a rural agricultural village.

In Dockside, Long Estate and Linton Bray there was greater segregation of the sexes and much stronger gender stereotyping than in Applegate. Clarricoates documents how the same behaviour was treated very differently in the schools. At Applegate one boy, Paul, liked to play with girls; he sought out their company and enjoyed their games. Tom and Edward in the same class liked playing ironing games in the play house. In Applegate this behaviour was acceptable; it caused no comment from teachers and other children were happy to play with these boys.

In the other three schools the same sorts of behaviour met a different response. Clarricoates observed that boys who chose to play in feminine areas of the classroom like the play house could find themselves being ridiculed and shunned by other children (Clarricoates, 1980a). In Long Estate there was a boy named Michael who really liked to play with dolls and with girls. He was constantly admonished by his teacher to try to 'behave properly'. She commented, 'Perhaps when he grows up he'll get straightened out' (Clarricoates, 1980a, p. 35). The head teacher of that school said she saw Michael's behaviour as a 'biological problem' (p. 36).

In different areas different values seemed to apply. Clarricoates suggests that different definitions of masculinity and femininity exist in these areas. In the working-class schools adults were desperate to suppress any identification with girls by young boys (p. 151; Browne and France, 1983, provide evidence of the same thing).

TEACHERS' CAREER PATTERNS

It is not only a question of what teachers do. The school is a social world, and men tend to have the positions of power in it. In Chapter 7 we discuss the question of teachers' careers in detail. Children see men in positions of power and women as carers and this gives them information about their own adult roles and likely destinies.

The evidence from research suggests that from nursery schools onwards through the primary education system, boys and girls are treated and talked to differently. In their early years they develop a sense of being boys or girls, and a sense that different things are expected from them in the context of this different treatment. Research work on the hidden curriculum alerts us to the fact that many messages about gender are transmitted in schools. In the ways they talk to, organize and treat children a social code is discernible. Teachers do not explicitly teach gender; it emerges in the curriculum, and both formal and hidden curriculum are involved.

CHILDREN'S INFORMAL CULTURE

It is also clear that children socialize each other in gender as well as other areas. Recent work by Davies (B. Davies, 1989) and Pollard (1985) has shed some light on the issue, but we have far more information on adolescent informal culture and on what goes on in secondary schools than we do for the early years. We will deal with the issue in more detail in the chapter on secondary education.

EXPLANATIONS AND THEORIES

It is important to look at the evidence we have presented in the context of the different and competing theories of gender socialization we outlined in Chapters 1 and 2. We must also ask what light this evidence sheds on the competing feminist theories. We do not want to go into these questions in any detail at this point, but will wait until we have presented the material on secondary schools as well, and can make a judgement on the entire story. However, it is clear that there is substantial evidence for the feminist position that schools create and reinforce gender divisions. We want to suggest that by the practices we have discussed schools may be contributing to the creation of different educational achievements between the sexes; and may be 'preparing boys and girls for a quite different style of life' (Deem, 1980, p. 1). As teachers we feel it is important that schools take responsibility for changing what processes and practices they can that affect girls' chances of fulfilling their individual potential.

CHAPTER SUMMARY

In this chapter we have looked at the way children's gender identification affects their learning and achievement. The process of learning to be male or female begins early in life in the family and is continued by the school. Within the school it is issues of school organization, curriculum and teaching method that seem to be particularly significant for primary school children. There is a range of different theories put forward to explain how these differences in achievement occur, and they relate to wider theoretical differences in approach to gender socialization and sex role stereotyping.

SUGGESTIONS FOR FURTHER READING

Nursery school

Browne, N. and France, P. (eds) (1986) *Untying the Apron Strings*. Milton Keynes: Open University Press.

Hodgeon, J. (1988) A Woman's World: A Report on a Project in Cleveland Nurseries on Sex Differentiation in the Early Years. Unpublished report available from Cleveland LEA.

Sylva, K., Roy, C. and Painter, M. (1980) *Childwatching at Playgroup and Nursery School*. London: Grant McIntyre.

Primary schools

Delamont, S. (1990) *Sex Roles and the School*. London: Routledge.

King, R. (1978) *All Things Bright and Beautiful?* Chichester: Wiley.

Curriculum

Assessment of Performance Unit (1982) *Mathematical Development: Primary Survey Report No. 3*. London: HMSO.

Cairns, J. and Inglis, B. (1989) A content analysis of ten popular history textbooks for primary schools with particular emphasis on the role of women. *Educational Review*, **41** (3), 221-6.

Lobban, G. (1975) Sex roles in Reading Schemes. *Education Review*, **27** (3), 202-10.

Sutherland, M.B. (1981) *Sex Bias in Education*. Oxford: Basil Blackwell.

CHAPTER 5

The experience of
secondary school

CHAPTER SUMMARY

This chapter looks at the way pupils experience secondary school. We look at the processes of sex role socialization in adolescence, and the way this affects pupils' reactions to school and in turn orients them towards the job market.

In this chapter we look at gender in the adolescent years. Feminists emphasize the fact that adolescence is an important phase in the processes of gender socialization and construction. Pupils go through adolescence in secondary school; it is a watershed and many aspects of the pupils' life in school are affected by the changes it brings.

The feminist argument is that schooling has a central role in creating, defining and reinforcing gender identity. This is true of secondary schools as well as primary ones, of course, and many of the processes involved are the same. In this chapter we look at gender socialization in secondary schools to understand how they frame and reinforce sex role learning in the adolescent years. The second issue explored is the way that children's experience of gender socialization affects their response to and their experience of school and ultimately their success or failure there.

GENDER AND ACHIEVEMENT IN SECONDARY SCHOOL

We have already discussed the fact that in primary schools girls do as well as or even better than boys. It is in secondary schools that girls, and particularly working-class girls, underachieve and fail. We need to identify why and how this happens. It is also the case that girls and boys underachieve in different areas of the curriculum. By the time pupils sit their first public examinations, differential subject special-ization has become firmly established and gender differences more pro-nounced (Willms and Kerr, 1987). Girls lean strongly towards the arts subjects and boys toward the sciences. We need to look at some of the factors that research has suggested are responsible for causing these problems.

Schooling for women's work

We have already suggested in this book that sex role socialization means that schools prepare each sex for quite different styles of life and places in life. Feminist writers from all theoretical approaches argue that in schools boys are oriented towards a lifetime of paid work and girls are oriented towards the home and child-rearing, or towards the kinds of job that are an extension of nurturing and home-making roles. Girls then leave school unqualified or underqualified for paid work in the labour market.

GENDER SOCIALIZATION AND ADOLESCENCE

Many of the processes of gender socialization and differentiation operate in both primary and secondary schools. However, some new issues emerge at secondary school, partly because pupils are reaching the new stage of adolescence in the life cycle.

Adolescence

Adolescence is a complex and contradictory stage of develop-ment. It is defined as 'That stage in the life cycle that begins at puberty and ends when the individual reaches maturity'. Naturally there are many definitions of maturity, but for the sake of convenience we may take the political definition, namely the age in Great Britain when young people are entitled to vote. (Coleman, 1980, p. vii)

There is an enormous body of research on adolescence that we cannot go into in any detail here. A number of different disciplines have made a contribution to our understanding of this stage of life. The chief approaches are the psychoanalytical, which concentrates on emotional developments in the adolescent, and the sociological, which concentrates on the social context in which adolescence takes place. In adolescence there are of course biological changes, but what we are most interested in are the ways individuals experience and make sense of these changes, and what meanings they attach to them. What we can say with some certainty is that adolescence is a time in the life cycle where a great deal of development takes place in a relatively short time. It can be a troubled time, but it need not always be.

The fact of their increasing maturity puts new issues on the agenda for pupils, and for teachers in secondary schools. Pupils begin to orient themselves towards the world of work and make choices about occupations and careers. This affects what they do in school. Adolescence is a time of identity change but future careers are not the only thing that is important. One of the key issues is the pupils' emerging sexuality. Schools have employed and evolved a range of responses and reactions to the complex and contradictory needs of pupils who are adolescents – some of which are more successful than others. In this chapter we will discuss the findings of feminist research into these issues.

THE EXPERIENCE OF SECONDARY SCHOOL

We have already identified school gender socialization processes in the chapter on primary education. Many continue to operate at secondary school level: school organization divides pupils for activities where gender is irrelevant and secondary school textbooks are as full of sex stereotypes as the primary ones, for example. To avoid repetition, we will not cover these issues again, but will aim to highlight those that are particularly significant in the secondary schools, and try to provide specific secondary school examples of these processes for those readers whose interests lie especially in this area. The issues we cover are:

1 The curriculum and subject choice.
2 Assessment and external examinations.
3 Teachers' actions and career patterns.
4 The hidden curriculum.
5 School career services.

CURRICULUM AND SUBJECT CHOICE

Secondary schools have traditionally offered a much more sex-segregated curriculum to pupils than primary schools. Before the introduction of the National Curriculum it was possible for pupils to be denied the opportunity to take certain subjects. Biology could be timetabled at the same time as physics in a school, for example, and this would mean that a child could not take both subjects. The National Curriculum could make a major impact here.

Sex-differentiated subject choice

The problem is that even when pupils are offered a full range of subjects, they continue to make sex-stereotyped choices. We have shown how this begins at primary and even at nursery level, but it reaches a peak in secondary school. Pupils come to see school subjects as being only suitable for one gender (Kelly, 1981; Harding, 1979). Table 5.1 illustrates the imbalances clearly, showing girls' preference for and success in English, history, languages and domestic and commercial subjects. The only science subject in which girls achieve the majority of passes is biology.

Table 5.1   Females as a percentage of CSE (Grade 1) and GCE 'O' and 'A' level passes: summer examinations, England and Wales, 1985

Subject	CSE(%)	GCE 'O' level (%)	GCE 'A' level (%)
Technical drawing	6.23	6.23	3.22
Physics	23.23	28.46	21.34
Computer studies	31.80	26.93	15.72
Chemistry	42.74	41.29	36.96
Geography	42.28	43.28	41.37
Maths	48.68	44.13	–
Maths, pure and applied	–	–	31.51
Economics	45.93	39.54	36.41
History	56.68	50.77	51.88
Art/Craft/Design	59.97	60.20	61.50
Commerce	62.30	–	–
Commercial subjects	–	57.10	
Biology	64.65	60.22	60.09
English	60.65	–	70.86
English language	–	56.74	
English literature	–	60.81	–
Social studies	68.74	–	–
Sociology	–	74.99	74.26
French	69.05	60.96	72.81
German	70.76	62.70	71.07
Business and office practice	90.35	–	–
Domestic subjects	95.71	–	98.90
Cookery	–	96.64	–
All subjects	*55.39*	*51.41*	*46.21*

Source: Department of Education and Science and Welsh Joint Education Committee.

Table 5.2   Percentage of school leavers with 'O' level/CSE* passes in given subjects, by sex, England, 1975/6 and 1984/5

	1975/6		1984/5	
	Girls	Boys	Girls	Boys
English	39	31	46	34
Maths	19	26	28	33
Science	20	20	26	35
Modern languages	17	12	21	13
Any subject	49	45	58	51

* GCE 'O' level grades A–C; CSE grade 1.
Source: Derived from Table CF, 'Statistics of Education, School Leavers, Jan. 1986' (compiled by Skeggs, 1989).

There are changes discernible in the figures for GCE and CSE passes over the last ten years (Table 5.2). Overall both girls and boys are increasing their pass rates in all subjects. For our purposes it is important to note that between 1975 and 1985 girls had increased success rates in maths (9 percentage points increase in 'O' level pass rate) and science (6 percentage points increase). The differentials may be decreasing. However, at the higher levels of attainment boys are still achieving proportionally far better results than girls in maths and science subjects. We look at the GCSE results for 1990 in Chapter 8 of this book.

Explanations

A number of explanations have been put forward for this imbalance. Genetic or biological ones assume that differences in ability and achievement are 'natural'. Those who accept social learning explanations emphasize the role of early socialization. Others blame the school and the ways teachers approach particular subjects. The explanations are basically the same as the ones we covered in the chapter on primary education.

However, there are some new factors in the social learning theories. So far we have looked only at the young child in the socialization theories, but we also need to consider what happens at adolescence. Social learning theories suggest that at puberty children are consumed with the concern to define their sex role identity, to establish themselves as masculine or feminine.

Some school subjects, notably science or at least physics and chemistry, are conventionally seen as masculine. There are, it seems, three main reasons for this: science qualifications are seen to lead to male jobs; the subject is seen as male dominated – more scientists are male, more science teachers are male; in addition, the subject itself is seen to be 'masculine' by school pupils. Ebutt asked third-year girls about their picture of women scientists. He reported that these were:

'Lots of thick glasses, flat shoes, big feet, judo types with muscular calves and sensible clothes. It is the flat chested flat heeled syndrome' (Ebutt, 1981, p. 20). Consequently girls tend to reject physical sciences as a part of their desire to be seen as 'feminine'. Science, like certain other areas of the school curriculum, has become invested with gender meanings. School subjects symbolise masculine and feminine characteristics, and pupils react to these. As Kelly puts it: 'Each sex, when educated with the other, is at puberty almost driven by developmental changes to use subject preference and where possible subject choice as a means of ascribing its sex role' (Kelly, 1981, p. 102).

Is the curriculum imbalance a problem?

We need to question whether this differential subject specialism matters. Those who accept a genetic or biological explanation for gender differences in ability and achievement do not see it as a problem. For them, different interests are 'natural' and the situation should be left alone. Feminists have argued against this position, and now there is support from government and official educational policy-makers for some change. The National Curriculum documents have put the issue on the agenda:

SCIENCE FOR ALL

Scope

7.1　It is our firm belief that all pupils should be able to benefit from their science education at school. However if this belief is to be realised in practice, and the attainment of all pupils improved, particular attention must be given to certain groups of pupils who, in the experience of their teachers and from the conclusions of research, often find it difficult to realise their full potential in Science.

7.2　These groups include girls, low attainers, gifted pupils, pupils from different ethnic backgrounds and those with special educational needs. Science for all is not yet a reality in many of our schools . . .

7.4　In the upper secondary years, boys tend to study Physics while girls take Biology. Many pupils therefore have an unbalanced, narrow scientific experience which ultimately constrains career opportunities and prospects for studying the separate sciences post-16. Both sexes are deprived of essential skills and knowledge and the nation's potential scientific resource is thereby diminished. (National Curriculum document: Science, DES, 1991)

We can see from this extract that there is official concern over the problem, which is seen to create difficulties for both the individual and the wider society. Sex-segregated subject specialism means that pupils are not receiving a full and balanced education; but this does not exhaust its implications.

The subjects pupils choose to study (together with the number of overall passes they gain) are important for securing entry into particular sectors of the labour market, and as a result have implications for pupils' careers and lives well beyond their school days. There is a gender division of knowledge within the education system, and the subjects in which girls predominate are not those which ensure entry into high-status occupations. By continuing to take these subjects, girls contribute towards making themselves unavailable for employment and training in which salaries and conditions are good.

Another problem is that in Britain in the 1990s there are all kinds of reason why women find themselves needing to enter paid employment. Divorce, male unemployment, inflation and the discovery that staying at home all the time with children is not idyllic are some explanations. The reality is that when women venture into paid work, they occupy a subordinate position in the labour market (Webb, 1989, p. 145). Some theorists have suggested that a dual labour market exists. There is a 'primary' sector in which available jobs are secure and well-paid, have promotion opportunities and are based on training and credentials. Then there is a 'secondary' sector where there is insecurity, little prospect of promotion, and low pay (Barron and Norris, 1976; Webb, 1989). Women are primarily employed in the secondary sector. Class of course plays a part; there are women in all the professions, but even here there are fewer women in the high-status posts. (See Chapter 7 for more details.)

Government concern over subject differentiation is largely based on economic considerations, for Britain has overall skills shortages in technical and scientific areas and needs women to make up the shortfall. The problem is not just girls and the sciences. Subject sex-segregation also means that boys leave school without good communication skills and without foreign language qualifications, and these are increasingly important in modern Europe.

The government's position is that this situation is unfortunate and unacceptable, and schools have been asked to introduce a range of curriculum innovations including compulsory science to remedy the situation. We introduced some of these initiatives, like TVEI, in Chapter 3, and will aim to assess them in detail in Chapter 8.

The official schemes are based on the assumption that once schools are aware of the problem and have information about it then they can solve it or at least improve the situation. Schools must provide equal access to the curriculum and offer all pupils the opportunity to take all subjects. The belief is that then girls as well as boys will take up these opportunities. The schemes also employ a control mechanism; with the compulsory core curriculum, pupils cannot opt out of particular subjects so easily.

Many liberal feminists are happy to support this approach, but others from the socialist and radical groups have been more critical of what is basically a reformist strategy. They argue that there is both direct and indirect pressures on pupils from within schools. Schools organize and differentiate between pupils in a variety of ways, they 'frame' notions of gender for pupils and they transmit a gender code. It is partly this gender code that directs pupils to make sex-stereotyped subject choices. Schools, then, help create the problem for girls. An effective remedy would require fundamental change in the practices and processes of schooling; the official schemes fail to offer this, and so will fail.

Conclusions

It is clear that the curriculum is an important area for those interested in gender equality in schools. The subjects pupils choose at secondary school have traditionally been sex-segregated, with profound consequences for both the pupil and the wider society. New schemes have been initiated to remedy this situation, but feminist critics have been doubtful of their aims and their ability to bring much real change. We will look in detail at the evidence for this criticism in Chapter 8.

ASSESSMENT AND EXTERNAL EXAMINATIONS

In recent years strategies of assessment have been researched by feminist thinkers (Murphy, 1989). They suggest that external examinations are sex biased and discriminate against girls. Many of the issues which they identify as problems are those we have already discussed in relation to the curriculum.

External examinations

In March 1985 the London GCE Board published a paper on bias and gender in their examination papers and expressed their concern about the bias against girls. Prompted by this paper, the Fawcett Society investigated all GCE papers for 1987, reading over 1,000 papers in all.

They discovered a number of problems, and argued that the examinations were not 'girl-friendly'; they did not take equal account of girls' interests and concerns. In all of the papers studied, boys' interests seemed to predominate. In mathematics, for example, 'questions are quite unnecessarily placed in contexts like football games or car engines' (Fawcett Society, 1987, p. 7). This is a problem because we know that the context in which mathematics is set affects how well women do it (Graf and Riddell, 1972). The Fawcett research also argued that women and girls in the maths papers appeared in stereotyped and frivolous contexts, with few examples of girls using their maths in an intelligent and sensible way.

Of the physical and computing sciences papers, the Fawcett researchers conclude 'There were few that would have been as interesting for girls as for boys' (p. 11). With only one exception all of the scientists named were male. 'The one exception was Marie Curie – the only woman scientist anyone ever seems to have heard of' (p. 13). The problem here is that we know girls are alienated by the 'maleness of science', which seems to be one of the factors that makes them decide it is not for them.

In both English and French literature papers, the problems were the same. Questions were set mainly on texts written by men. Where Bronte's *The Tenant of Wildfell Hall* was examined by AEB, none of the questions involved female characters. In English language papers, the composition topics were more male oriented than female; prose extracts too were written by men and likely to appeal to boys' interests (p. 18). In 1978 Walters looked at the sex of writers of prescribed 'A' level texts for the summer examinations (Table 5.3). The Fawcett research makes it clear that very little had changed in the intervening time.

Table 5.3   Sex of writers of prescribed 'A' level texts, summer examinations 1978

Board	Women writers	Men writers
London University	1	26
AEB	0	15
Metropolitan Board	1	10

Source: Walters, 1978, p. 7.

In history papers the questions emphasized military and diplomatic history, ignoring much social history and women's role in history. The same pattern was true for social studies, and the Fawcett Society singles out law papers as being a particular problem. The one exception to this picture is home economics, where the discrimination is reversed, and there was very little to interest boys.

There are special problems in some curriculum areas. Bradberry (1989) looked in detail at GCE 'O' level mathematics papers. He noted the poor performance of girls in comparison to boys overall, and also pointed out that girls performed significantly less well on particular topics than boys, and that there were some topics in which the reverse was true. Bradberry makes a telling point: mathematics papers test the topics on which boys do better than girls more often than the topics on which girls do well. There is a question of bias in the selection of topics in examination papers (Bradberry, 1989).

Research is beginning to make it clear that multiple-choice questions favour boys (Murphy, 1981; Harding, 1979). The explanation for this is probably that girls do better when they are given a detailed and relevant context to a problem. Examiners report that girls frequently focus on irrelevant details in the brief, multiple-choice question and reach the wrong conclusions as a result. It seems to be the case that boys do better when there is not such a context (Graf and Riddell, 1972). Criticisms are made of physical science and computing papers for favouring the multiple-choice type of question. The answer would seem to be to offer more of a choice to everyone.

Conclusions

The evidence is that external examination papers contain bias and contribute to girls' underachievement. We know from research on the curriculum that pupils fail to engage with certain learning opportunities on the basis of gender. 'What they judge to be appropriate they tackle with confidence. What they consider alien they avoid' (Murphy, 1989, p. 38). The feminist argument is that examinations must offer a fair range of activities and topics so that neither sex is disadvantaged by them. Bias needs to be eliminated; at the moment the evidence is that external examinations favour boys.

The Fawcett Society commented that now the 'O' level examinations have been superseded by the GCSE, the hope is that the new boards will take on the equal opportunities issues more effectively. The society is currently monitoring the GCSE work.

Classroom assessment

Goddard-Spear's research raises another matter. She casts serious doubt on the objectivity of teachers. Teachers were asked to grade a piece of science writing; when told the writing had been done by a boy they graded it more highly than when they were told it had been done by a girl (Goddard-Spear, 1989). Clearly this is an area in which we need wider-ranging research to find out how common a problem this is.

TEACHERS' ACTIONS AND CAREER PATTERNS

Teachers as role models

We will discuss this issue in detail in the chapter on teachers' careers, but there is a new factor which comes into play in secondary education and which is worth mentioning here. Male teachers dominate the school subjects that girls do badly in, like the sciences. It means that girls have few models of successful women in these curriculum areas. One of the arguments that those who support single-sex schooling make is that in single-sex schools there is more likelihood of women teachers holding these positions. When we turn to the issue of teachers' actions, there are three main factors: teachers give more attention to boys, prioritize their interests and encourage them more in the classroom.

Inequality in teacher time and attention

In primary education it is clear that boys are able to dominate teachers' time and attention. The evidence is that they continue to do so in secondary schools. This information is now well enough known for it to be included in the concerns of a secondary school principal in the *Neighbours* television series (11 June 1991).

Boys' potential to disrupt lessons seems to be even greater in secondary schools than it is in primary:

> Boys are the source of the fun and the laughter, but also of the confusion in the classroom. The dynamics of the classroom are radically affected by the presence of boys. Even a seasoned teacher can be dictated to by the dominant elements of the class. (Spender and Sarah, 1980, p. 121)

Study after study shows boys receiving the greater share of teacher time and attention (Galton, 1981; Stanworth, 1981; Spender, 1982; Wood, 1984; Mahony, 1985).

Lesson content

There is evidence of secondary school teachers developing lesson content to appeal to boys' interests. Elliot (1974) found he faced disruption from the boys otherwise. When girls were not interested they would daydream or chatter; they might not be working hard, but they did not disrupt the class in the same way as the boys, so it was easier to ignore them. Shaw (1980) states that the way boys' interests are privileged makes mixed schools more like boys' schools. She suggests that such processes have the effect of lowering the girls' self-esteem at school (see also Stanworth, 1983, p. 19). They feel they do not count as much as boys (Draper, 1992).

Verbal input and gender

One issue that has been seen as important in feminist literature is that of girls' verbal participation in classes. The pattern of non-participation develops clearly by the secondary stage of schooling: 'Women don't talk as much as men in mixed company, and girls don't talk as much as boys in mixed classrooms' (Spender and Sarah, 1980, p. 148). The stereotype is that women talk a lot, but feminists point out that women do not talk much in public, when a large number of people are listening to them. Women's talk belongs to private arenas. (For a full discussion of this issue see Corson, forthcoming.)

It seems that this affects the classroom behaviour of both pupils and teachers. John Elliot (1974) noted that while a few girls were willing to take part in classroom discussions the majority were not. There is evidence also of boys shutting girls up. Research findings on secondary school classrooms reveal that teachers permit boys to talk more and encourage them to challenge and question more than girls, and that their talk is evaluated differently. Researchers have watched teachers in the classroom talking to boys and girls. Girls are discouraged from talking a lot through a number of non-verbal and verbal means. Gaze aversion is one of these mechanisms; if someone is talking and we look away, we give her/him a signal to stop. Withholding of active listening responses like nods or requests for elaboration also operates in the same way. Interruptions curtail verbal participation too, and we know that girls do get interrupted more than boys (Zimmerman and West, 1975). Teachers may not be aware that they are doing any of these things. Sadker and Sadker (1982) showed teachers a film of a classroom, asking them to say who was talking more. The teachers overwhelmingly said the girls; in reality the boys in the film were out-talking the girls at a ratio of 3:1.

This pattern of behaviour has important implications for learning and achievement. Barnes (1976) makes it clear that learning is an active process. We do not learn by osmosis; new information needs to be 'talked into place'. If there are social pressures in classrooms on girls not to talk, then there are pressures which inhibit their learning and contribute to their underachievement.

Conclusions

There is evidence that by their actions, some of which they may not be aware of, teachers communicate important messages about sex roles and school achievement to both girls and boys in schools. We now go on to look at the fourth important issue we identified at the beginning of the chapter: the hidden curriculum.

HIDDEN CURRICULUM

In the chapter on primary schools we identified the range of ways that the hidden curriculum operates to transmit a social code. Feminist researchers have suggested that schools communicate messages about what kind of behaviour it is appropriate for girls to engage in. Clarricoates, for instance, found that teachers assumed that boys would be more lively and adventurous, independent and energetic (1980); girls by contrast were obedient, tidy, conscientious and gossipy. Study after study indicates that teachers put greater pressure on girls to be quiet, neat, careful and demure (Ingelby and Cooper, 1974; Deem, 1978; Delamont, 1990). It is arguable that much of the material we have discussed in the previous section on teacher actions and attitudes reveals powerful messages in the hidden curriculum.

The processes which transmit the hidden curriculum are the same in primary and secondary schools. Teachers' language and anecdotes are again a source of gender 'messages', and the jokes and banter that they use in the classroom and corridors have the same function. We will look at these first in this section. However, the content of the messages in the social code changes at this stage of schooling, and we also need to look at the ways that schools deal with the issues of adolescent sexuality.

Classroom management strategies

In the chapter on primary education we discussed the way that some teachers may use gender as a way of organizing classrooms, managing lessons, motivating pupils and keeping discipline (Delamont, 1990). In secondary school teachers continue to differentiate between children on the basis of gender. Buswell (1981) noted that in one classroom she studied, pupils were classified by sex up to twenty times a day. One example of what teachers do is taken from our research into science lessons; the teacher would always welcome his class with the words, 'Come in my merry MEN' (Measor, 1984).

Our research unearthed many examples of teachers setting boys and girls in competition with each other. In a CDT lesson, the task was to make a water-bearing container from stiffened paper. As a motivational strategy the teacher said, 'Come on girls, I want you to beat the boys hollow on this.' The teacher repeated the comment several times throughout the course of the lesson (Measor and Woods, 1984).

We have already suggested that research makes it clear that teachers' choice of curriculum examples often relate more to boys' interests than to girls'. This example from a science lesson on measurement shows how boys' interests are privileged, with important consequences for them; but it also indicates other 'hidden curriculum' messages too:

> The teacher dealt with heat, measured by thermometers, with liquids measured in pints like beer and gallons like petrol. The teacher then went on to question whether any of the children had ever gone to France by car. This illustrated the difficulties caused by different forms of measurement; and the teacher questioned how their FATHERS dealt with litres and kilometers. 'Have none of you got adventurous dads that took the car to France?' (Measor, 1984, p. 187)

The social class models implied in this teacher's comment are interesting in themselves, but there are important gender implications too: of passive mothers who are taken places, if they are lucky.

Many teachers use banter in a way that makes gender framing points. The same science teacher, discussing electricity and conductivity, warned, 'So the moral is if you are wearing nylons, don't step on electric wire, because you'll get a nasty shock up your backside' (Measor, 1984, p. 187; see also Delamont, 1980, p. 58).

Teachers may exchange a range of 'asides', comments to pupils that have the same role. We have already discussed the CDT lesson in which the teacher used competition between the sexes as a motivational strategy. In this way he seemed to be saying that girls could be as good as boys at this subject, which they saw as being 'for the boys'. However, in between his exhortations to excel, the male teacher carried on a loud conversation with some male pupils about how dreadful women drivers are. It is important to question which part of his teaching carried most weight.

Social codes for boys and girls

One of the times we can discern the content of the social code in the hidden curriculum is when an individual breaks it and is reprimanded. There are some clear pictures in the research of what happens to girls who do not conform to the picture of a 'proper' girl. Parker reported the strong disapproval teachers gave to girls who were seen to be 'loud' and 'aggressive' (Parker, 1976). Sadker and Sadker (1982) suggest that boys are allowed to be much more assertive in these areas than girls.

Llewellyn (1980) describes the way that teachers dealt with one particularly 'difficult' girl named Sandy. Sandy was seen to be a problem because she was 'difficult' in the classroom, showing little motivation toward school work. In addition she initiated contact and conversation with the boys in her school, she was sexually explicit and she had a 'big mouth'. She met with a great deal of disapproval, from both staff and other pupils, and she was disliked and isolated. Llewellyn provides an account of one incident, where a senior teacher said to Sandy: 'Just calm down Sandy; with a temper like yours, my girl, you'll be lucky if you get a husband' (p. 48). Ball (1981), Davies (L. Davies, 1984) and Measor and Woods (1984) provide similar accounts from different schools. In the following chapter we show the way that other pupils cope with girls like Sandy.

Sexuality

Sexuality is one of the key issues here, and in the last few years there has been an increasing amount of research done on the dynamics of sexuality in secondary schools (Prendergast and Prout, 1987; Fine, 1988; Wolpe, 1989; Holly, 1989). The researchers concentrate on two main issues, the teaching of sex education and the sexual harassment of girls in school.

Much of the analysis focuses on the ways that schools teach sex education, suggesting that this offers insights into the way they deal with sexuality generally. The most common pattern is that schools teach the biological facts of reproduction and contraception, and include material about sexually transmitted diseases – it is a 'plumbing and prevention approach' (Lenskyj, 1990). In the current situation schools are having to undertake AIDS education, and that introduces new pressures and themes (Holly, 1989). Schools provide 'knowledge' about the mechanics of sex and the processes of reproduction. There is little or no provision made for dealing with the emotional elements. Pupils note this and have expressed their dissatisfaction (Allen, 1987).

In addition it seems that school sex education does not frame itself around the realities of adolescent sexuality (Measor, 1989). In a school one of us researched there was a fresh, hearty, open-air approach to human sexuality, the human body and reproduction. However, from observation of the pupils it seemed that the world of adolescent sexuality was rather different, and the sex education failed to take their needs and culture into account. Again pupils expressed their dissatisfaction with this approach. A number of research studies have made one issue clear, that adolescent girls would prefer to be taught sex education in single-sex groups (Halson, 1989; Measor, 1989; Swetman, 1989).

In the light of this evidence it is possible to suggest that sex education is failing to meet the expressed needs of adolescent pupils. Fine, for example, suggested that this leaves young women vulnerable:

> The adolescent woman herself assumes a dual consciousness at once taken with the excitement of anticipated sexuality and consumed with anxiety and worry. While too few safe spaces exist for adolescent women's exploration of sexual subjectivities, there are all too many dangerous spots for their exploitation. (Fine, 1988, p. 35)

Feminist writers have argued that schools aim to control sexuality and particularly female sexuality in a number of ways (Wolpe, 1989). They point out that teaching about sex is usually underpinned by material about marriage and the family. The 1986 Education Act provides guidelines for schools, stating: 'Where sex education is given . . . it is given in such a manner as to encourage those pupils to have due regard to moral considerations and the value of family life' (Section 531, No. 7). This and other legislation means that homosexuality is now a difficult matter for schools to teach, and treating the issue with any sympathy is problematic in the current context. The 1986 guidelines also encourage schools to deal with sexual morality, and discuss the dangers and difficulties of promiscuity and premarital conception.

The problem for feminists here is not that schools deal with this material – it is clearly important that pupils have the facts and are aware of the health dangers that face them. It is that schools teach a different moral code on sexuality for boys and for girls. 'Boys are not expected to be chaste before marriage, quite the contrary' (Wolpe, 1989, p. 120). Girls, however, are. Schools confirm the double standard, and give clear messages to girls about their sexual responsibilities.

Some feminist writers have taken this argument about the control of female sexuality further. Radical and psychoanalytic feminists have reflected on the way that women's sexuality is framed and have described it as being 'passive'. They argue that in our society women feel like the objects of male sexuality, with little sense of their own rights to sexuality and perhaps even less sense of what their own desires are. MacKinnon describes women's sexuality as 'that which is most one's own and yet most taken away' (MacKinnon, 1983, p. 227). Women therefore do not have a sense of their autonomous sexuality.

This affects their relationships with men in a negative way, but the effects do not stop there; radical feminists suggest it can affect their whole sense of autonomy, independence and ability to succeed in the world (Baker Miller, 1986).

The suggestion is that schools have a crucial role to play in these processes of constructing and controlling women's sexuality. Radical and psychoanalytic feminist theories are by definition radical, and are currently in the process of being worked out; they do not form part of mainstream thinking on education; and yet they are making some important claims, and so need to be considered by those who are likely to be responsible for children's sex education.

Sexual harassment in schools

The other major issue that has concerned feminists is sexual harassment. Sexual harassment is difficult to define, but it covers 'any repeated and unwanted comments, looks, suggestions or physical contact that might create a stressful or intimidating working environment, or threaten a woman's job security' (Sedley and Benn, 1982, p. 6).

Both women teachers and female pupils are exposed to sexual harassment. Teachers are harassed by male colleagues and also by male pupils (we discuss this in more detail in Chapter 7). There is evidence that girls are subject to substantial sexual harassment, largely from boys in the school, but sometimes from their teachers too (Mahony, 1985; Lees, 1986; Herbert, 1989; Holly, 1989). Halson (1989) gives an account of a teacher who caused girls both discomfort and embarrassment. They called him Mr Casanova. Carol Jones (1985) spent nine months in a large London comprehensive researching sexual harassment in school. She comments, 'Male teachers were quite open about their attitudes towards the girls, often putting their arms around the girls and making comments such as you're looking gorgeous today' (p. 29). In Lynda Measor's research into Old Town comprehensive she witnessed some similar incidents; one male teacher would walk down corridors with his arms around older girls, addressing one girl, whose name was Erica, as 'Hi Erotica' (see also Draper, 1992).

By and large, however, the evidence is that while teachers create embarrassment for girls, it is male pupils at the school who act in ways to cause girls humiliation. There is considerable verbal abuse. Girls are taunted with a series of names: 'slag' is perhaps the habitual and universal epithet, though 'bitch', 'dog' and 'lez' (lesbian) are also common. The effect of such labelling can be profound (Lees, 1986). Boys comment on girls' appearance: 'As girls walked into the class groups of boys jeered, commented on the size of girls' breasts and their appearance' (Jones, 1985). Direct sexual harassment is also common, with boys sliding fingers down girls' backs and lifting their skirts, or pretending or attempting to do so. 'Girls are leered at in classrooms and "felt up" or groped as they walk about' (Halson, 1989). Girls referred to this as '"being got" by the lads' (Halson, 1989). There is substantial evidence that sexual abuse is so common that it comes to be accepted as part of ordinary life in school. There are few examples of schools seriously trying to limit the abuse that goes on (Mahony, 1985, is an exception). There is evidence that the abuse distresses girls, who we would argue have a right to be protected.

Conclusions

The hidden curriculum, then, transmits a number of messages about the appropriate way for adolescents to behave in school and in the community, and also in their personal lives and relationships. Teachers differentiate between pupils on the basis of gender and suggest that different social codes apply to them. Boys and girls receive different messages from the way their sexuality is treated in school.

SCHOOL CAREERS SERVICES

The careers service of a school also has a role to play. Although there is now a considerable literature on gender inequality in education and in employment there is virtually no research on the careers service which bridges the two (Breakwell and Weinberger, 1987; Cockburn, 1987; Eden and Aubrey, 1988, are the exceptions). The Women in Science and Engineering Campaign (WISE, 1984) revealed to the EOC the extent of the inadequacy of careers information inside schools. It is clear too that girls are often given misleading and inaccurate information about employment opportunities open to them.

In 1988 new guidelines on providing a vocational service were produced by the Department of Education and Science. They specifically indicated that the careers service must promote equal opportunities. In a recent article Coles and Maynard (1990) publish their findings on how much the careers service has done to develop new programmes to fulfil the equal opportunities objectives.

Only 55 per cent of careers services had a specific policy on equal opportunities in place. Others hinted that this was not really a priority issue. Many services had no written guidelines for implementing equal opportunities policies in their day-to-day work – in advertising vacancies, for example. Frequently there was no named senior officer who had responsibilities for equal opportunities. Overall there was a lack of funding for in-service training in the field.

EXPLANATIONS AND THEORIES: AN OVERALL ASSESSMENT

At this point, with the evidence from both primary and secondary school, it is important to assess the different and competing theories of gender socialization we outlined in Chapters 1 and 2 of this book. The basic feminist argument is that gender differences are not all 'natural', but are constructed by elaborate socialization.

From the data we have presented here it is clear that schools at every level of the education system are involved in practices and processes which treat boys and girls differently. Schools use gender as an organizing principle and operate to differentiate between children. While we cannot know for certain what is determined by 'nature' and what is constructed by 'nurture', we can discern a great many activities in schools and in the family which direct children into different patterns and experiences according to their gender, and can argue that this must affect the ways they play, work and think about themselves and the world.

In Chapter 2 we discussed the controversies which exist between liberal, socialist and radical feminist accounts of education. A further question is what light the evidence that we have presented sheds on the competing feminist theories.

Radical feminist writers concentrate on power relationships between boys and girls in schools. Classroom research makes it clear that boys dominate girls in the classroom and secure greater attention than them, leaving the girls at a disadvantage. Recent research on nursery schools indicates how early these patterns of inequality begin. At secondary school boys continue to receive more of the teachers' time, interest and attention and their interests are privileged. In addition there is substantial evidence that boys engage in sexual harassment of girls and female teachers. While it is difficult to judge the entire argument about patriarchy on the basis of classroom data of this kind, nevertheless it supports the radical feminist argument that some boys dominate schools and classrooms and reduce girls' chances of success at school by their activities.

However, we need to moderate the argument, for as Wolpe points out (1989) not all boys are noisy, demanding of the teacher's attention, and likely to harass girls. Some boys may do this, but there are widespread differences in the way boys behave – they do not all do the same things. Wolpe is concerned to get a more accurate picture of what goes on in classrooms, but she also has a theoretical point to make. She feels it is important to note that schools fail many working-class boys in exactly the same way they fail girls. We need, in her view, to take account of class as much as gender in our attempt to understand schools. Others like Connell agree, and also insist on the importance of 'race' (Connell, 1989). The argument about boys' domination of the classroom is at the heart of the dispute between radical and socialist feminists, about whether men and, by extension, patriarchy are the major cause of gender inequality, or whether class and, by extension, the capitalist system are most fundamentally responsible.

Socialist feminism draws our attention to the larger social context in which schools function, and to the role of schools in selecting children and allocating them to particular occupational categories. In this view schools are also involved in justifying this selection process. The socialist feminist argument starts from the position that schools are responsible for creating social inequality, and gender inequality is one aspect of this.

There is a huge weight of evidence that schools are involved in reproducing traditional gender roles. Research into nursery and primary schools indicates that boys and girls have a range of different experiences there which directs them towards different activities in school. The argument is that these activities have the potential for directing children into quite different roles and later adult occupations.

At secondary school these processes continue. Socialist feminists emphasize the importance of the curriculum subjects pupils study at school, which act as a foundation for the later division of labour in the workforce. The process of subject choice is an important one because it sets the direction of future life chances and careers for pupils. The issue is seen as being at the heart of the process by which working-class girls underachieve in our society and are schooled for 'women's work'.

In the view of the socialist feminists, working-class girls learn their future position as low-paid earners in the workforce as a result of the way they are treated in school. In addition, they internalize their position as subordinate to men through the processes of differentiation in school: 'Girls are trained in school in skills which are appropriate to this division of labour, they are also trained that this division of labour is natural' (Spender and Sarah, 1980, p. 34).

There is evidence that girls are disadvantaged at school and that they face discrimination in some areas as a result of assumptions that are made about their interests in school and their aspirations for careers after school. Girls are also disadvantaged by the classroom domination of and the harassment by boys in schools. While the evidence we have discussed in this chapter cannot answer some of the larger theoretical questions about social systems, education and capitalism, nevertheless it is clear that girls do not get a 'fair deal' in the great majority of schools, and that their experience in school fails to encourage girls to develop to the best of their potential.

The evidence also reveals that the way children are treated in school is influenced by larger social constraints. We can trace the influence of gender, class and 'race' on their experience of school and on their likely progress in it. The evidence we have presented in the chapters on primary and secondary education does offer support for the feminist approach which sees schools creating sex role and gender differences. The question remains of the degree of responsibility that schools have as opposed to other social agencies. Our own view is that there are many factors at work: school, home, the community and the mass media all have a role to play in the construction of sex stereotypes. However, the research does suggest that schools play a significant part in these processes of creating gender divisions and educational inequalities between boys and girls.

It is important to emphasize that schools and teachers are not the only factor at play in this context. Pupil attitudes are important too, and in adolescence pupils begin to make decisions for themselves. The next chapter deals with this issue in detail.

CONCLUSIONS

In this chapter we have tried to look at the reasons for the under-achievement of girls, and particularly working-class girls, in our schools. We have drawn attention to the impact that society and the mass media have on the situation, and the effect that schools and teachers have too, together with the ways that schools are organized and run. What we have left out of this account is the effect that adolescent culture has upon girls' achievement in schools, and this will be the subject of the following chapter.

There is, however, one more important point to make. We have in this chapter looked in some detail at the kinds of message that pupils receive in school. The next question is how pupils receive them and respond to them, for not all pupils will respond in the same way.

CHAPTER SUMMARY

In this chapter we have looked at the sex role socialization that goes on in secondary schools and we have tried to link the processes with those of primary school. As pupils enter adolescence they meet a number of new pressures and opportunities, and begin to make decisions that will affect their adult lives and careers. As a result of the way they organize and teach adolescents, schools seem to give them a number of messages about the directions and the opportunities they should take. These messages vary with the pupils' gender, social class and 'race'.

SUGGESTIONS FOR FURTHER READING

Adolescence

Coleman, J.C. (1980) *The Nature of Adolescence*. London: Methuen.

Gender and schooling

Arnot, M. (1984) How shall we educate our sons? In R. Deem (ed.), *Co-Education Reconsidered*. Milton Keynes: Open University Press. This is an interesting analysis of how the kinds of segregation and differentiation process that we have discussed in this chapter affect boys, and it contains suggestions about ways forward. It is highly theoretical in parts.

Deem, R. (1980) *Schooling for Women's Work*. London: Routledge & Kegan Paul.

Delamont, S. (1990) *Sex Roles and the School* (2nd Edition). London: Methuen. This is an introductory account which is very accessible to readers new to the field.

Spender, D. and Sarah, E. (eds) (1980) *Learning to Lose*. London: Women's Press.

Stanworth, M. (1983) *Gender and Schooling*. London: Hutchinson.

The journal *Gender and Education* is a useful source for very up-to-date research material. The journal aims to make the majority of its articles accessible to non-specialist readers.

Girls and the sciences

Kelly, A. (1981) *The Missing Half*. Manchester: Manchester University Press. This is a comprehensive introduction to the major issues in this field.

Examinations and assessment

Murphy, P. and Moon, R. (eds) (1990) *Developments in Learning and Assessment*. Milton Keynes: Open University Press.

Murphy, P. and Johnson, S. (1986) *Girls and Physics: Reflections on APU Survey Findings*. London: HMSO.

Walters, A. (1978) Women Writers and Prescribed Texts. *Waste Papers*, presented at the National Association for the Teaching of English, Annual Conference, York.

CHAPTER 6

Secondary school:
informal interaction

CHAPTER OVERVIEW

In this chapter we look at the ways that pupils socialize each other in secondary school, where peer group culture becomes important. We also look at the youth cultures which adolescent pupils develop and the role these can play in pupils' attitudes to school, suggesting they are involved in the failure and underachievement of some groups.

So far we have concentrated on what schools do to pupils. We have outlined the processes of gender socialization and the mechanisms by which schools select pupils and allocate them to particular roles in life. Families and the mass media also clearly have a role to play in both these processes. However, there is another important ingredient, and that is other pupils. We want to argue that pupil-to-pupil relationships and peer networks are a major component of a child's experience of schooling.

It is useful to make a distinction between formal and informal aspects of school. By 'formal' we mean 'that aspect of pupil experience and career that relates to goals, values and organisation specified by teachers in the school acting in their formal capacities'. By 'informal' we mean 'the aims and values that exist apart from the formal, best expressed through the peer group or "teen-age" culture' (Measor and Woods, 1984, p. 3). Research evidence makes it clear that pupils develop an informal culture of their own. In recent years there has been a lot of research into the informal culture and the kinds of behaviour and attitude that pupils develop in it.

The two cultures intermingle, sometimes harmoniously and some-times with conflict. Teachers impose the formal culture on pupils, set-ting its parameters and defining its criteria, and pupils react in a variety of ways to it. Pupils also attempt to impose their informal culture on teachers, which can be a cause of conflict.

The research indicates the strength of the effects of youth cultures upon at least some adolescents, and suggests that they are one of the chief social mechanisms through which learning does or does not take place. By choosing in this chapter to concentrate on adolescents, we do not intend to suggest that informal culture is not important to primary school children. It clearly is, but we want to suggest that the informal cultures of childhood are rather different from adolescent cultures, and that informal cultures play a different role at the adoles-cent stage of the life cycle.

In this chapter we want to consider the role informal adolescent cultures play in gender socialization and then look more widely at the effects they can have upon pupils' attitudes and responses to school.

FRIENDSHIP GROUPS

The starting point in any discussion of informal culture is the friend-ship groups that pupils form. From the 1960s researchers began to indicate the influence and importance of friendship groups in the lives of adolescents. In the previous chapter we discussed some of the characteristics of adolescence, and stressed that it is a period in the life cycle when a great deal of development takes place in a relatively short time. One of the major thrusts of this development is that children begin to establish themselves as independent beings and to move away from their family. Emotional bonds with parents stretch, change and weaken. Friends come to occupy the space that is left and fulfil a vitally important emotional and social role for the young person. Adolescent friendships, therefore, are intense because they carry a heavy developmental load.

Until the 1970s the majority of the research on friendship groups in school was on boys. More recently we have acquired similar levels of knowledge about girls. There is a very large literature on this issue, and while we will make reference to some of the material on boys, our main focus of interest will be girls. Both girls and boys form groups which are equally important to them. However, it is clear that there are crucial differences between boys' and girls' groups.

Girls' groups are smaller than boys'. Henry (1963) noted, 'boys flock, girls seldom get together in groups of above four' (Murdock and Phelps, 1973; McRobbie, 1978b, backed up these observations). The other related issue is that the 'girls' groups are more intimate than the boys'' (Blyth, 1960, p. 139). This intimacy is an important matter. The suggestion is that girls' groups involve greater emotional intensity than boys'. Girls seem to offer warmth and support to each other in their groups, and this is a very important factor for the adolescent in coping with school. 'Our data suggests that these relationships were for girls almost a complete life-support system' (Measor and Woods, 1984, p. 166; see also Llewellyn, 1980; Meyenn, 1980).

However, this emotional intensity does not only involve warmth and support. A number of authors have described and been perplexed by the negative emotional turmoil that seems to characterize groups of girls, and it is an issue which concerns many teachers in their daily school lives. Girls were seen to be 'always having arguments, and falling out' (L. Davies, 1984, p. 10). They were always 'making friends' and 'breaking up' with them (Meyenn, 1980; B. Davies, 1982; Measor and Woods, 1984; Nilan, 1991). This may simply be a part of the general emotional turmoil of adolescence. However, research has suggested that some of these 'makings and breakings' of friendship groups are connected with gender socialization processes.

FRIENDSHIP GROUPS AND GENDER SOCIALIZATION

Feminist research has suggested that friendship groups act as agents of socialization in general and gender socialization in particular (Llewellyn, 1980; Measor and Woods, 1984; Lees, 1986; Nilan, 1991). Messages about what it means to be a girl or a boy and how to behave in adolescent culture are both transmitted and enforced by children in these groups. Social and normative rules govern the members of the friendship group. The female groups seem to operate with a 'moral sense' of what it means to be a 'proper' girl, and this implies a certain set of behaviours and attitudes. If these norms are broken then sanctions can be applied by girls in the group (Measor and Woods, 1984).

Llewellyn has shown how wide a range of behaviour the groups cover (1980). For our purposes the most important issue is the code which sets out what is appropriate behaviour for girls in school (Measor and Woods, 1984). The major issues covered by the code seem to be appearance, sexuality and attitudes to school. We will deal with appearance and sexuality first and with attitudes to school in the next section.

Appearance

Appearance is a key issue. The code of femininity states that girls must take appropriate care with their appearance and be conscious of fashion and style. However, it is important they do not take this too far. This is associated with a more general issue of presentation of self, which demands that girls are quiet and unassuming.

In Measor and Woods (1984), we suggested that the code led to disapproval for girls who were anything other than demure and moderate. We observed pupils offering bitter criticism to others if their skirts were too tight or their make-up anything but discreet. We also observed the distress this disapproval caused (Measor and Woods, 1984, p. 101). Criticism was not restricted to the girls' friendship groups: if girls did not heed the warnings given by their own friends, they could find censure coming from older girls in the school and also faced disapproval from boys.

Sexuality

The main issue was, however, sexuality, for as Sara Delamont comments, 'Nice girls don't' (Delamont, 1990, p. 49). Feminist research has made it clear that a double standard is alive and well among adolescents in schools. While there is no expectation that boys should be either chaste or faithful, girls are expected to be both:

> Liz: Look I don't believe there should be one standard for a boy and another for a girl. But there is round here, and there's not much you can do about it. A chap's going to look for someone who hasn't had it off with every bloke. So as soon as you let him put a leg over you, you've got a bad name. (L.S. Smith, 1978, p. 37)

A girl's reputation is extremely important and must be maintained and guarded at all cost. The research makes it clear that girls are not allowed to be sexual; the appropriate behaviour is 'romantic silliness' (Delamont, 1990, p. 48). The code is enforced by the group. Any girl who breaks the code on what counts as appropriate sexual behaviour faces criticism and unpleasantness. In the most 'serious' cases, Nilan (1991) shows that particular girls were excluded from their friendship groups. However, before it comes to this there are various early warnings, and we suggest that many of the 'makings and breakings' that we referred to earlier are examples of such sanctions being imposed on girls who have failed to stay within the rules.

Membership of a friendship group in school seems to be extremely important to girls and is invested with emotional intensity. Being excluded therefore counts a great deal. Group members spend significant amounts of time together, both in and sometimes out of school. They do many things together, and 'being with your friend' is most important (B. Davies, 1982, p. 77). To lose a friend or be denied membership of the friendship group is a serious matter for most adolescents.

In the previous chapter we described how teachers can disapprove of girls who do not conform to appropriate codes of behaviour. There is evidence that other girls share these perspectives, and censure from peers can be far more damning and damaging. In our research (Measor and Woods, 1984), we watched the progress of a girl, Shirley, who broke all the rules of the 'code'. She began by minor infringements, wearing too much make-up and clothes that branded her as a 'tart'. She was constantly in trouble at school. But there were far worse things as well. She was given the label of 'hard', a characteristic usually attributed to boys:

Claire: She is one of the worst girls I have ever known.
Jenny: She is really disgusting. (Measor and Woods, 1984, p. 153)

The problem was her sexuality. Shirley 'went out with' boys who were much older than she was, and during her first year at school she became pregnant and had an abortion. Her reputation was gone and she became vulnerable as a result. At the end of that year she was assaulted by a group of boys in a lonely part of the school. They stood around her in a circle and made her take off most of her clothes while they engaged in games of touching, teasing and threatening her. At a local disco she was again surrounded by a group of boys who made her remove her clothes.

The story was well known around the school and it operated as a warning to the other girls. The kinds of penalty that can be applied to a girl who entirely loses her reputation are graphically illustrated in this account. Shirley played a dual role in 'policing the boundaries' of the gender code (Llewellyn, 1980). On the one hand she stood as a symbol of everything a proper girl should not do. In this way she was a threat, representing a challenge to the girls' widely held norms. Conversely she was also a source of comfort; their picture of her constantly reinforced their own female standing.

Conclusions

Research into friendship groups makes it clear that they transmit and enforce a number of rules about behaviour and attitudes. It is important to note that any message about gender or sex role differentiation propagated by school will be filtered through the informal culture of the group, and group membership can give the adolescent substantial support to defy the school culture.

It is the case, of course, that different groups have different norms and values (Llewellyn, 1980). The differences in values may be connected to social class and the pupil's place in the school's academic hierarchy. The girls' groups made judgements about each other and about their teachers in relation to these norms.

We now need to turn to the other important issue in the code: attitude to school. The fact that different groups have different values and attitudes is of decisive importance in this context.

DEVIANCE AND RESISTANCE

Gender socialization is not the only issue at stake in the informal culture. We also need to look at the pupils' experience of the formal culture of the school and their response to it. There is clear evidence that pupils do not approve of all they are given in schools, and that some of them rebel and react against it, engaging in disruption and deviance.

Researchers generally have been fascinated by this area of pupil life and culture, and have drawn a great deal of attention to it. Marxist sociology has invested it with special meanings, which we must look at in more detail later in this chapter.

Deviance

'The central fact of deviance is that it is created by society. Social groups create deviants by making the rules, whose infraction constitutes deviance and by applying those rules to particular people and labeling them as outsiders' (Becker, 1963, p. 131).

In schools, we can say deviance is about breaking the official and unofficial rules of the institution. In the classroom it is about disrupting lessons, defying teachers and causing 'trouble'. Deviance may also take the form of passive resistance or withdrawal.

Lynn Davies lists a wide variety of offences in school. They range from 'chatting in class' to 'setting fire to something', with a wide range of 'messing about' behaviour in between. (1984, p. 87). There is evidence too that different kinds of school provoke different kinds of deviance, which seems to be related to the structure of the school – for example, whether it is streamed – and to its general ethos.

Girls and deviance

Until recently we knew almost nothing about girls' deviance in school, for they were invisible in the research. Boys' deviance, by contrast, had received substantial attention (Hargreaves, 1967; Lacey, 1970; P. Willis, 1977). The evidence we have now suggests that when girls show their objections to school, they do so in rather different ways from boys.

In Chapter 4 we discussed the fact that primary school teachers generally see girls as being more conformist. At secondary school, research suggests that 'girls, are overall still seen as being less disruptive, violent or delinquent' than boys (L. Davies, 1984, p. 6). Yet girls are not always seen as easier to control and motivate than boys. Teachers see girls as engaging in particular types of delinquency. It is important to note that over time teachers find that these acts can cause far more serious difficulties than the things boys do.

Part of the problem lies in the relationships girls have with teachers. Girls do cause teachers trouble in class, but it is their response to the attempt to discipline them that seems to cause the greatest difficulties (L. Davies, 1984, p. 11). Girls in Davies' research were seen to be impertinent, unwilling to accept discipline, quick to take offence and likely to hold grudges against teachers for a long time.

Our research backs this up (Measor and Woods, 1984). Teachers at Old Town recognized the problem of 'girls getting upset' if they were 'told off', and they dreaded these reactions. It's 'Light the blue touch paper . . . and remember to stand back basically.' The headteacher commented, 'I'm always picking up the pieces. You get flocks of girls going round to complain to their head of house about Mr. X or Mr. Y.' (Measor and Woods, 1984). This meant that many teachers, especially male ones, found problems in knowing what strategies to use in disciplining girls. This in turn gave the girls some power and some safety from trouble in school (Measor and Woods, 1984, p. 117).

There are implications for teachers in this research data. Different policies and discipline strategies may need to be worked out for dealing with girls. Government initiatives like the Elton Report (DES, 1989d) which offered new approaches to discipline do not really emphasize the gender issues, and during initial training students are probably given more preparation and ideas about dealing with the kind of disruption that boys present. Girls' deviance tends to be more passive, and this may be an important element in the construction of a properly feminine identity. Research suggests that deviance is connected with and intersects with youth culture, and can create very significant consequences for pupils' attitudes to school and for their achievement there.

DEVIANCE AND ADOLESCENT YOUTH CULTURE

The starting point here is a definition of culture and subculture. Youth cultures are usually seen to be a type of subculture.

Culture and Subculture

We understand the word 'culture' to refer to that level at which social groups develop distinct patterns of life, and give expressive form to their social and material life-experiences. Culture acts as a kind of blueprint for behaviour and feelings, and contains hints on norms and rules to observe.

The pre-requisite for the formation of a subculture is a group of people with a common problem, thrown together in a common situation, who then find a common solution. Through dress, activities, leisure pursuits and life style they develop a different culture to the main culture of the society.

Subcultures must exhibit a distinctive enough shape and structure to make them different from the main or dominant culture of the society. (Hall and Jefferson, 1976, p. 10)

The argument is that deviant pupils form into groups in school and develop a culture which is anti-school. They object to and avoid schoolwork, reject teachers' standards and values, dress in styles the school does not approve of and have no wish for academic success. Such pupils are also likely to engage in specific leisure activities and favour particular pop music that defines them as a group. Hargreaves (1967) and others have pointed out that adherence to anti-school peer group norms will be stronger than any pressure that school and teachers can exert. Membership of and adherence to the norms and values of a deviant group can make a difference to the school attainment of pupils, and can lead to underachievement.

The theory was first developed in the context of white working-class boys at secondary school. Hargreaves (1967) and Lacey (1970) noted that these boys formed themselves into groups in school. The most important issue differentiating the groups was attitude to school. Boys who showed little commitment to school work or to school norms were responsible for much of the disruption and deviance in the classroom. Their low performance was linked with other characteristics, like sexual precocity, 'trendiness' and a generally high level of interest in youth culture. A decade later Ball (1981) identified many of the same processes, and confirmed that they were still going on in comprehensive schools.

The next question that we need to ask is whether these same processes operate for girls in school. Feminist research has established that the pattern is similar, although girls have their own forms of deviancy. The female non-academic counter-culture is expressed in distinctive forms of dress and values, and equally ensures under-achievement and failure (McRobbie and Garber, 1976; Llewellyn, 1980; Meyenn, 1980; L. Davies 1984). We still know less about the girls' youth cultures than we do about the boys, and this is an area in which we need more research (McRobbie and Garber, 1976; Robins and Cohen, 1978).

It is important to try to establish the characteristics of the girls who 'turn off' school. Ball noted that the lower-band girls in the compre-hensive school he researched were far more interested in fashion, pop music and culture than were those in the top band. The latter seemed to combine their interest in teenage culture with a determination to continue to do well in school (Ball, 1981). McRobbie and Garber (1976) found essentially the same processes at work. In 'Mill Lane' school the deviant girls formed a group which saw themselves as 'naturally' having an antagonistic relationship with the groups of girls who con-formed to what school wanted. They referred to them as 'the swots and the snobs' and were contemptuous of their willingness to work hard at school. In Measor and Woods (1984) we observed the same phenomena, but suggested that there were 'three broad categories amongst pupils, conformists, deviants and those who walked a thin line between on a "knife edge"' (p. 139).

If we look at the kinds of pupil who 'turn off' school, a number of factors emerge as important. Individual matters, like personality and family, are clearly significant. However, social class and 'race' seem also to have a significant effect. Middle-class children are perhaps generally more pro-school. Even if they dislike what school offers and demands from them, none the less they use it instrumentally to gain qualifications for the future (Delamont, 1976; Lambart 1976; Ball, 1981; Aggleton and Whitty, 1985, show the same processes at work for boys). There is also a suggestion that some groups of black girls may behave in a similar way (Fuller, 1980; Mac an Ghaill, 1988).

EXPLANATIONS

There are significant numbers of girls who 'turn off' school, and enter deviant youth culture groups. Most frequently they are working-class. Working-class boys do the same thing, but feminist research has alerted us to the fact that the explanations for girls' actions may be different from those applying to boys.

We will deal with some of the most significant of the explana-tions that have been put forward to account for this process. Firstly we look at the rational choice model, where girls are seen to be choos-ing a 'natural' and traditional option for themselves. Secondly we dis-cuss the developmental theories which see girls' choices being made in response to life cycle pressures. We will then focus on a range of sociological theories which stress that girls switch off from school as a reaction to their discomfort at failure there. We will explore next the suggestion that girls may fear academic success as a threat to their femininity. Finally we will deal with the various strands of Marxist argument that suggest we need to take account of wider social and economic factors when we seek to explain what happens to working-class girls in the education system.

Rational choice model

It may be that girls never lose sight of the fact that there is always another job for women apart from paid work. They do not see their future as one in which they are permanent members of the paid labour force. They accept the messages they get from home, school and the mass media which suggest a home-based role for women. It seems natural to them to accept the traditional female role. Education therefore has very little value for them.

Study after study demonstrates girls displaying this attitude (Dove, 1975; Sharpe, 1976; Llewellyn, 1980; L. Davies, 1984). The girls in Sharpe's research saw no point in doing well at school or staying on at school. They said they had no interest in getting good jobs after school; they wanted to marry and have children. Our data, collected in 1983 with 13-year-old girls, illustrates some of the issues involved. The girls expressed their opposition to the idea of women choosing jobs and careers instead of marriage and children. They were clear that it was not as important for girls to have jobs when they left school as it was for boys, 'because girls can do the housework and boys have got to get the money' (Measor and Woods, 1984, p. 154). For these girls jobs were not the prime concern; the focus was on marriage and babies:

JANIE   I want some children, loads of them . . . a couple of little babies all cuddly.
RESEARCHER   Do you ever think it would be boring to have kids and just be at home all day with them?
JANIE   No, you can play with them and that, and they can help you do the cooking like jam tarts.
JACQUI   I should think they would be ever so sweet. (Measor and Woods, 1984, p. 154)

In the rational choice model the girls' actions and attitudes are defined as a matter of choice; these girls are not interested in what school has to offer. The argument is essentially a conservative one, which rests on the assumption that providing equal opportunities for everyone is all that is necessary to change the situation. The argument fails to recognize the pressures that can result in pupils not being able to take up these opportunities. The argument also has connections with sociobiology and with the view that gender differentiation is a 'natural' thing.

Developmental perspective

An alternative explanation suggests that girls at this stage in their lives are interested primarily in developing their identity as feminine (Kelly, 1981). It may be that school offers different goals from this, which as a result do not appeal to girls very much. School may also seem to reduce their ability to explore and develop this femininity. Sharpe points out that there may not be very much connection for girls between their growing sense of womanhood and their lives at the average school. They therefore react against school as an irrelevant aspect of life that they nevertheless are unable to escape.

A number of authors have suggested that sexuality is involved in this process. 'One of the causal factors in the low level of achievement in academic terms appears to be the effect of erupting sexuality on pupils' lives' (Wolpe, 1989, p. 97). Wolpe shows a number of ways in which schools fail to acknowledge this effectively (1989). She criticizes the formal curriculum of schools, especially in the area of sex education. (This is an issue that we looked at in detail in Chapter 5.) There are difficulties in interpersonal relationships between peers, but also between pupils and teachers. Other problems arise from the ways schools insist on dress and other rules. School uniform, for example, is often very masculine and, as Payne comments, 'could not have been better designed to disguise any hint of adolescent sexuality' (Payne, 1980, p. 14). School rules which ban make-up, jewellery and nail varnish also work to create rule infringement among girls (King, 1978). The girls disobey school rules in order to do the things they value and are interested in. At a general level Wolpe asserts, 'Recognition and acceptance that sexuality plays an important part in the lives of adolescents is not apparent', and this is responsible for some of the academic problems that arise for particular groups of girls (Wolpe, 1989).

The developmental theory is similar to the rational choice perspective in that the school's goals are seen as irrelevant. The girls' deviance is understood as an attempt to adapt the school's regime into something that offers more scope for their interest (McRobbie and Garber, 1976). Hostility to school stems from their perception of the school goals as irrelevant. It is femininity that counts. The model is a useful one, for it draws our attention to the pupils' perspective on school and enables us to see things from their point of view. However, there are difficulties with this theory, for it cannot explain why it is working-class girls who seem to be most affected by these developmental imperatives.

Deviance as a reaction to failure

There are a number of other arguments, which depend upon different sociological theories of deviance. One line of thinking suggests that deviant, anti-school girls want to hit back at a system which has branded them as failures. The label causes discomfort and distress and girls try to avoid the distress in a number of ways. They may use the fact of being a girl as a means to escape from the pressure to be academically successful. They retreat into the safer domain of marriage and domesticity, which they assert provides greater fulfilment.

Girls may also seek to avoid distress by creating a different status hierarchy, with different criteria of success from the formal academic ones. In his research Ball (1981) suggested that for the lower-band girls allegiance to adolescent culture provided an alternative route for status and identity. They turned school values upside down, and by smoking, cheeking teachers and 'skiving off' they gained prestige. This contest is one where the terms are more favourable to them, and which offers them a greater chance of success (L. Davies, 1984, p. 166).

In this theory, the girls are seen to be reacting to failure to achieve school goals rather than finding them irrelevant. Therefore hostility to school derives from frustration at being denied access to the goals of the school. A number of researchers have pointed out that although the alternative culture the girls create draws a lot from a commercial teenage culture, it also reflects a traditional working-class value system, or to be more accurate what we know of the working-class value system (L. Davies, 1984, p. 170).

The theory has a lot to recommend it. In Chapter 1 we looked at the role schools have in selecting and allocating pupils. We also looked at the unfairness that seems to be involved. It is likely that the working out of these processes creates some reactions in pupils. Working-class children who are failing in school engage in rebellion and deviance. Davies puts it in the following way: 'Schools are not socialisation agencies; they are colonising agencies. It is hardly surprising that there will be resistance to this colonisation, especially when it acts in the interests only of the potential tribal leaders' (L. Davies, 1984, p. 127).

Fear of success and femininity

Other approaches have concentrated on the suggestion that girls in general, but working-class girls in particular, judge academic success as being 'unfeminine'. The assumption is the traditional one that 'bluestockings' do not find husbands or boyfriends, and will fail as women.

Research from America has demonstrated that women can fear academic success (Horner, 1971). In an experiment college students were asked to finish off a story in which a girl came top of her year in medical school. The women students wrote stories in which the girl in the story, while she was successful in later life, met with a series of personal tragedies, was isolated, lonely and – unmarried.

Horner's work is American and it was done in the 1970s, and it is tempting to dismiss it on the grounds that times have changed and things are different over here. Yet her work does suggest something highly controversial; that is, that we still have trouble reconciling ambition, competence, intellectual accomplishment and success with femininity (Spender and Sarah, 1980). The argument is that girls at adolescence may feel they are faced with the choice of deciding whether to opt for achievement or popularity. They fear that maximizing their achievement will bring disapproval. The threat within our society is that as successful women they will face a lonely and unattached existence (Spender and Sarah, 1980, p. 151). Girls may well find it far more threatening to be unfeminine than to be unsuccessful.

The data we gathered in Measor and Woods (1984) supports the argument that girls, especially those from working-class backgrounds, may feel threatened by academic success, especially perhaps in mixed comprehensive schools. Academically confident and successful girls in our research found other pupils very critical of them, and faced a range of difficulties. They were isolated and had few friends.

The data have similarities to Willis' material (P. Willis, 1977). In Willis' work, the conformist boys, the 'ear-oles', were seen as being less sexual and less sexually competent by the deviant working-class 'lads'. Their identity as 'men' was in question. It seems as if the same holds true for working-class girls who are placed in the highly conformist category by other pupils. Their sexuality is in question and their identity as feminine is suspect as a result of academic success.

There is British evidence about the way that boys and later men view academically successful women. It seems clear that boys place pressure on girls in school. Fenema comments, 'Most boys don't want girls to do better than them in school work' (Spender and Sarah, 1980, p. 60). This was certainly the case for the boys we researched. They did not see 'brainy' girls as desirable 'objects', and said they would not want to go out with 'a brainy girl'.

RAY Who wants to go out with a brainy girl? It would make you look a real idiot – a real brainbox. I wouldn't fancy that anyhow. (Measor and Woods, 1984, p. 155)

These attitudes were extended into their view of their adult life. Boys in the research did not like the idea of having a wife who had better

103

qualifications than they did and they were especially disapproving of the idea of being married to a woman who earned more than them.

Such research is useful because it demonstrates some of the pressures that apply to working-class pupils in school. Success in school has different meanings and implications for them and for middle-class pupils. The research is also important because it indicates the effect that class has upon codes of what counts as masculine or feminine behaviour. If definitions of masculine and feminine can vary in this way then there are implications for any suggestion that gender is a fixed and 'natural' category. Such research adds weight to the feminist case that gender is socially constructed.

Marxist theories

Marxist feminists in their explanation draw our attention to the larger social and economic system in which gender is constructed. In Chapter 2 we discussed the Marxist view that working-class girls are exposed to a double load of oppression, as members of the working class and then additionally as women.

Schools are involved in reproducing these inequalities. Sharpe (1976), for example, points out that the values and attitudes involved in sex role differentiation do not develop in an arbitrary way; they are influenced by the economic structure of society and its economic needs. She emphasizes the division of labour and the need for women to form a reserve army of labour that can be employed and laid off at will. Researchers in this tradition go on to suggest that working-class girls have some sense that this process of reproduction of an unequal society goes on in school. If these girls see schools as places where middle-class values rule, and where working-class children fail and are seen to fail, then they may react against them. This perspective may not be well formed or clear, but it motivates action nevertheless.

Marxist and socialist feminist theories stress the fact that both girls and boys resist these processes as best they can; they do not just accept the imposition of unequal chances in the class system quietly. So these writers suggest that working-class girls resist schooling on the basis of a 'class instinct'. In this theory deviance is seen as a response to a wider process of class and gender oppression.

Winning consent

In Chapter 5 we discussed recent Marxist work which has argued that schools do not force or coerce pupils into a subordinate role but rather manage to win consent for the allocation process. Willis' work was important in this context (P. Willis, 1977). He studied a group of anti-school, deviant, working-class boys, who lived in a traditional industrial town. He suggested that working-class boys expressed a class-based hostility to schooling through the development of alternative 'style' and a fascination with heavy industrial work. The boys' resistance to school meant that they ended up getting, and most significantly wanting, working-class jobs. They rejected school and sneered at the conformist pupils, the 'ear-oles' who tried to succeed in school. For these deviant 'lads', making an effort in school was not an option, because it represented a threat to their masculinity. Maleness for them was defined in a large part by the successful handling of a manual job in heavy industry.

The central thrust of Willis' argument is that all of the strategies of resistance employed by boys in their subcultures are, in the final analysis, self-defeating. Willis studied only boys and drew the wrath of feminists as a result. If we apply the analysis to working-class girls who are involved in deviant youth cultures the end result is the same as it is for the boys: they leave school without the qualifications that will give them access to middle-class jobs, status and life chances.

However, this is not clear to those who are 'inside' the subculture and deeply involved in its strategies and styles of resistance. To them the subculture represents a bid for freedom and a rejection of the oppressive traditions of school. McRobbie argues that subcultures

> illustrate the contradictions in so-called oppositional activities. Are the girls in the end not simply doing what is required of them – and if this is the case, then could it not be convincingly argued that it is their own culture itself which is the most effective agent of social control for girls, pushing them into compliance with that role which capitalist society directs them towards. (McRobbie, 1978b, p. 15)

Allegiance to deviant youth culture and its subcultures means the adolescent engages with style and develops a fascination with various leisure activities. This seems to promise a freedom from the depressing realities of being at the bottom of the pile in capitalist society. The freedom is illusory: the reality is that girls accept the domination of both class and gender. Moreover, in their subculture girls invert the hierarchy of productive over domestic labour which we are used to in capitalist society. They escape to the domestic world and celebrate its confines. As a result they leave the division of labour unchallenged and with it the hierarchy of male over female.

All of these arguments are dependent on the Marxist view of capitalism, and of the role of schools within that system. Capitalism is seen as an oppressive and exploitative system, which disadvantages working-class people. Schools have an important role in reproducing that disadvantage across the generations. In this view schools are seen as an agency which is very tightly tied to capitalism. Deviance on the part of working-class pupils is therefore seen as important because it is a signal that the group which is most disadvantaged by capitalism is resisting its oppression, and there is hope for change in the system as a result. Deviance, then, is seen in this theory as a reaction to over-whelming odds, and as a political matter.

The theories have been criticized, for they seem to suggest that all working-class children are involved in highly colourful and exciting youth cultures and that all pupils are polarized into the groups we have discussed. The problem is that the argument fails to take account of the large numbers of children who drift through school, either alone and not a member of a group at all, or simply not challenging anything. As a result they perhaps get very little out of school. Academic failure in school does not always result in active resistance to school or to the growth of subcultures (Ball, 1981).

Willis' work virtually ignored girls' perspectives, and much of the Marxist subculture research has been criticized because it glamorizes a 'macho' culture and leaves girls invisible. We applied the theory directly to girls, but it is important to note that there are integral problems with any theory which is formulated on data gathered on only one gender.

CONCLUSION

In this chapter we have aimed to discuss the main areas in which informal culture is important in schools. We looked first at the area of friendship groups and the ways that female pupils divide themselves up into different groups. The groups have an important role to play in gender socialization, communicating messages about what it means to be a proper girl and enforcing that code. Some of these groups become involved in deviant activities at school; they begin to develop an anti-school orientation and 'turn off' school. For some working-class deviant pupils the values and activities of the adolescent youth culture become more important than any school values. In this way working-class pupils find themselves leaving school without the qualifications that open up middle-class occupations and life chances. This seems to be true of both boys and girls. Adolescent culture is clearly more important to some groups of pupils than it is to others, and involvement in informal adolescent cultures has unequal consequences, affecting working-class pupils more and in more significant ways than it does the middle-class. However, 'race' and gender are other important variables in this process and in the way that pupils work out their own life chances in school.

CHAPTER SUMMARY

In this chapter we have looked at the importance of the informal culture for pupils in school. The informal culture carries messages

about gender and also about attitudes to school. Working-class children seem particularly likely to object to what school offers and demands of them, and to develop an anti-school culture which has profound effects upon their achievement levels at school.

SUGGESTIONS FOR FURTHER READING

Youth cultures

Marsland, D. (1983) Youth. In A. Hartnett, (ed.) *The Social Sciences in Educational Studies*. London: Heinemann. A useful review of the literature on youth which collects material together in an accessible form. However, despite the development of new research on girls, Marsland only reviews material relating to boys.

Mungham, G. and Pearson, G. (1976) *Working Class Youth Cultures*. London: Routledge & Kegan Paul. A useful introduction to the debate on youth cultures, this book has the advantage that it does not see youth culture as a single unit, but emphasizes the impact of class and ethnic identity. However, there is no material in the book on gender. The same is true of Hall and Jefferson (1976).

Willis, P. (1977) *Learning to Labour*. Farnborough: Saxon House. This is a key book in this area of adolescence and informal culture. The first section is an interesting account of working-class boys' groups. The section of analysis, which is taken from a Marxist point of view, is rather theoretical.

Girls and deviance in schools

Davies, L. (1984) *Pupil Power: Deviance and Gender in School*. Lewes: Falmer. A full and useful account of the way that girls show their objections to school and some of the consequences this can have for them.

Fuller, M. (1980) Black girls in a London comprehensive school. In R. Deem (ed.), *Schooling for Women's Work*. London: Routledge & Kegan Paul.

Griffith, C. (1985) *Typical Girls*. London: Routledge & Kegan Paul.

Llewellyn, M. (1980) Studying girls at school: the implications of confusion. In R. Deem (ed.), *Schooling for Women's Work*. London: Routledge & Kegan Paul.

McRobbie, A. and Garber, J. (1976) Girls and subcultures. In S. Hall *et al.* (eds), *Resistance through Rituals*. London: Hutchinson.

Open University (1981) Popular Culture, Class and Schooling. *Unit 9, E353, Society, Education and the State*. Milton Keynes: Open University Press.

Girls' youth cultures and schooling

McRobbie, A. (1980) Settling accounts with subculture: a feminist critique. *Screen Education*, **34**, 37–49.

McRobbie, A. and Nava, M. (eds) (1984) *Gender and Generation*. London: Macmillan.

CHAPTER 7

Teachers' careers and gender

When a woman teacher enters school she brings with her not only her professional skills and experience, but also herself as a person. Since school cannot be separated from society at large, society's power structures remain as significant within the school community as outside. Sex, race, class, and to a lesser extent sexuality are important factors influencing the way women are viewed and treated.
(De Lyon and Widdowson Migniuolo, 1989, p. 113)

CHAPTER OVERVIEW

In this chapter we want to shift the emphasis away from pupils and on to teachers in order to look at some of the ways in which women teachers experience teaching as a career. We shall be focusing particularly on the following:

1 Women teachers' place in the career structure.
2 Women teachers and promotion.
3 Women teachers' experiences in school.
4 Gender in initial teacher education (ITE).
5 Gender in in-service teacher education.

WOMEN TEACHERS' PLACE IN THE CAREER STRUCTURE

Teaching is a good job for a woman but a career with prospects for men.
(H. Burgess, 1989, p. 90)

In Chapter 1 we discussed the fact that there is substantial inequality between men and women in our society. In the majority of occupations women are dramatically under-represented in senior and high-status positions and, therefore, earn on average less than men (EOC, 1990). In medicine, for example, in 1986, only 0.6 per cent of general surgery consultants were women and even in obstetrics and gynaecology, 'women's areas', they held only 12 per cent of consultancy posts (*Guardian*, 14 November 1989). The situation in higher education is similar, with women holding only 3 per cent of professorial posts and 6 per cent of senior lectureships (Hansard, 1990).

More men than women hold academic posts in universities (24,578 men compared to 3,025 women: Hansard, 1990), but in teaching women are in the majority. The figures for 1986 show that the full-time teaching force in English and Welsh state primary and secondary schools was made up of 245,100 women and 156,790 men (DES, 1989a). Nevertheless men occupied a greater, and consequently a disproportionate, number of senior positions. Indeed, in 1988, in English secondary schools a male teacher was about three times more likely to receive the top D or E incentive allowance than was a woman (DES, 1989b). Table 7.1 shows the figures relating to head and deputy headships and scale 1 posts (the career structure has been changed since these figures were collected; scale 1 now falls within the Main Professional Grade).

The number of promotion posts available in any school is linked to the number and age of its pupils. Secondary schools, therefore, tend to have more senior posts than primary schools. Since the majority of primary school teachers are women their opportunities are obviously more limited than their secondary colleagues, yet, even here, as Table 7.1 reveals, men dominate. What might some of the reasons for this be?

Table 7.1 Numbers and percentages of female and male heads, deputy heads and scale 1 teachers, England and Wales 1986

	Head	Deputy head	Scale 1	All
Primary				
Men: (number)	11,575	7,168	3,594	35,947
(%)	32%	20%	10%	*
Women: (number)	9,683	11,066	52,565	138,329
(%)	7%	8%	38%	*
Secondary				
Men: (number)	3,625	6,042	20,543	120,843
(%)	3%	5%	17%	*
Women: (number)	843	2,135	39,505	106,771
(%)	1%	2%	37%	*

* Totals for percentages are not 100 because the table does not include figures for those in scales 2, 3 and 4 and senior teacher positions.
Source: DES, 1989a.

WOMEN TEACHERS AND PROMOTION

During the 1920s and 1930s the majority of LEAs used the idea that men were the 'breadwinners' to vindicate the imposition of marriage bars which prohibited the employment of married women teachers. These bars were not officially repealed until the 1944 Education Act. The notion that men had dependents to support and so needed a higher salary, whereas women were financially supported by their husbands and consequently only worked for 'pin money', was used up until 1961 to justify higher pay for men. Then, in 1961, an equal pay agreement was implemented after a long, persistent and bitter fight (see Partington, 1976). This agreement represented something of a coup because at the time, fourteen years before the Sex Discrimination Act (1975), differential pay for men and women doing the same or an equivalent job was the rule rather than the exception, as it still is in fact if not in law (EOC, 1990). The argument that men are the 'breadwinners' failed to take into account single teachers of both sexes, and worked for the benefit of men and detriment of women.

Today, theoretically, teaching is a career in which women and men enjoy equal opportunities. As we have seen, however, even though the basic salary is the same for men and for women, male teachers on average continue to earn more than their female counterparts because a higher proportion of them occupy the senior positions which carry more money. Various explanations have been put forward as to why more men are in promotion posts. On the whole, however, these explanations are inadequate because they are frequently based on assumptions which are taken for granted – on what Sara Delamont describes as 'staffroom folklore' (Delamont, 1990, p. 83) rather than research-based data (for further discussion see NUT/EOC, 1980; Acker, 1983, 1989; Davidson, 1985; Kant, 1985; Evetts, 1989). Feminists argue that they focus on reasons which hold women responsible (such as, 'women are not as persistent in their applications', 'women are not as committed'), instead of addressing the socially pervasive structural sexism which is at the root of the matter. Nevertheless, given the lack of sufficient data to confirm or disprove their veracity, these 'myths or folkbeliefs, . . . are probably having long-term consequences for the lives of women teachers' (Delamont, 1990, p. 84).

We will now look at some of the explanations put forward by feminists as to why proportionately fewer women occupy senior positions.

Assumptions about women teachers' commitment

It is argued that there is still a strong feeling within society that the proper and prime role for a woman is that of wife, mother and carer. In this view occupational careers should come second, and it is often assumed that women will and should always put their family first – taking time out to have and raise children and time off to look after sick relatives, resigning and moving when their partner gets a job in another part of the country – whereas men's commitment will and should be primarily to their career (see R. Burgess, 1988). Such assumptions may influence decisions about whom to appoint and promote (Kant, 1985; R. Burgess, 1988).

Suspicion about the degree of commitment which could be expected of married women in general and mothers in particular has led to reluctance to appoint young and unmarried women. This is not lessened by the way in which teaching appears to fit in with family life, since at first glance it might seem that mother teachers only work the same hours that their children are in school. In the course of our own (unpublished) research teachers have told us of their experiences at interviews. For example:

> 'They asked me if I was engaged and when I was thinking of getting married, and one of them even asked if I was planning to have any children' (woman teacher talking of interview in early 1970).
>
> 'I was very naive when I first got the job (as headteacher). I remember being horrified the first time I was involved in appointing a teacher. We'd interviewed all the candidates and were discussing them over a cup of tea and the chair of the governors said "Well, that Miss [X] we can rule her out because she's a good looking bit of stuff and it won't be long before she's married and into child-bearing. No she's a bad bet." I thought what am I involved in? Anyway she was plainly the best and I wanted her and the other governors agreed with me. But he wasn't pleased' (female headteacher).

Although blatant questions about domestic circumstances and plans have been illegal since the passing of the Sex Discrimination Act (1975), it is impossible to legislate against the influence of beliefs that are taken for granted.

One of the most commonly given reasons to explain women teachers' lower status is that they take time out in order to have and raise children and thereby both lack experience and get left behind on the career ladder. However, studies which discovered that 60 per cent of women secondary teachers in Warwickshire did not have children (Smith and Bells, 1989), and that nationally 30 per cent of women teachers over 50 were childless (NUT/EOC, 1980), mean that

> at any point in time, the 'average' woman teacher is as likely as not to be childless. Such figures make a mockery about married women popping in and out of the profession in accordance with the needs of their families. (NUT/EOC, 1980, p. 24)

Similarly Davidson (1985), Grant (R. Grant, 1987) and Evetts (1989) all found that women tended to take nowhere near as much time out of service as was commonly believed. Nor are arguments that women's domestic commitments prevent them from being involved in the extra-curricular activities and the out-of-school time courses that are believed to help in the promotion stakes (Lyons, 1981) supported by the evidence (see Davidson, 1985, p. 200).

Assumptions about commitment are misleading and have negative implications for men as well as women. Indeed, what little data there is suggests that commitment to their family acts as just as much of a disincentive for promotion for men as it does for women (B. Hughes *et al.*, 1976; Sikes, Measor and Woods, 1985; Sikes, 1986).

Assumptions about women's lack of ambition and persistence

In 1974 Hilsum and Start published data which indicated that men were more persistent in applying for senior posts than were women. They instanced men who had applied for up to a hundred headships and women who gave up after four rejections. Feminists have argued that if it is the case that, generally speaking, women are less persistent, it may be because female socialization tends not to develop the same sorts of attitude, sources of satisfaction, self-perceptions and self-confidence that male socialization does. This could mean that women are more likely to doubt their ability, aptitude and suitability for senior positions, and that any rejections will serve to confirm these doubts.

Hilsum and Start (1974) and various surveys undertaken by LEAs have found that, for senior posts in general and secondary school headships and deputy headships in particular, male applicants far outnumber females. This has been interpreted as women being less ambitious. However, the NUT/EOC (1980) research and Davidson (1985) found little difference between women's and men's ambitions; it was just that women felt that their chances of success were poorer.

Teaching for pocket money

As we have already noted, differential pay has been justified on the grounds that men have families to support. But then so do women. There are a growing number of single-parent families in which the mother is the main breadwinner – and some of these mothers are teachers. For example (from our research):

> 'I got married too young, I'd got no idea what it would be like. Anyway we stayed together till the children were both at school and then decided to separate. I needed a full-time job because I wanted to take over the house and the mortgage. I need the money and I could obviously do with the extra I'd get from a promotion. I know a lot of other women teachers who're in the same boat' (Ann).

Other women support elderly relatives, so the idea that men have a special case for promotion and extra pay is clearly not that straightforward.

Assumptions that men are better disciplinarians

Feminists have been critical of what they see as a general belief that a man will be better equipped to deal with the perceived problems of schools in 'rough' areas. This is linked with the notion that with older children it is more appropriate and necessary to have a man at the top in order to maintain discipline (see Davidson, 1985). Therefore men gain headship posts. These beliefs are based on a conceptualization of management based on force and control, and on a view of women as physically weak and men as powerful authority figures. It has been suggested (for example, Shakeshaft, 1986; Al-Khalifa, 1989; De Lyon and Migniuolo 1989) that there are other ways of creating an ordered climate and men as well as women may prefer to use these 'alternative' approaches.

Women's under-representation in high-status areas

There are fewer women teachers working in the high-status and shortage subject areas, in particular maths and physics, which offer a greater number of incentive allowances and senior posts. Research into teachers' career perceptions and experiences, conducted by Alan Marr and Maggie MacClure, found that:

> As many as a third of teachers, mainly women, are caught in a trap where schools give incentive allowances and in-service training to teachers with extra responsibilities . . . In secondary schools, posts of extra responsibility are given to retain teachers of shortage subjects, who are mainly men. In the primary sector, most of the teachers are women and there are just too few incentive allowances. (*Times Educational Supplement*, 12 October 1990)

This state of affairs creates a vicious circle because practically all deputy headships and headships go to people who are already in senior jobs. This means that because women are less likely to obtain head of department and faculty type positions they stand less chance of reaching the 'top' management jobs.

Women, networks and sponsors

Women are less likely than men to be plugged in to social networks which arise from membership of male-dominated or exclusively male societies like the Round Table, the Knights of St Columba, the Freemasons, sports clubs, political parties and trade unions (see P. Hughes, 1989). They are also less likely to acquire what Geoffrey Lyons (1981) calls 'career sponsors' among the senior staff in their schools, not least because there are few women in senior positions (see Rumbold, 1990). Although it is difficult to prove, membership of social networks and sponsorship are both believed to be likely to enhance an individual's career prospects (Hilsum and Start, 1974; Morgan, Hall and McKay, 1983; Sikes, 1986; R. Grant, 1989).

The effects of reorganization

The comprehensive reorganization of state secondary education led to the abolition of many single-sex schools. It was usual for girls' schools to have a female head and to be staffed predominantly by women; men similarly held the monopoly in boys' schools. Co-educational schools, however, are generally headed by men, with men occupying the majority of senior posts. This has meant that an important source of promotion and seniority for women has been lost. The increasing tendency to combine separate infant/first and junior schools to create large primaries has also had the effect of reducing female representation at head level, because whereas it was almost unheard of to have a male infant school head, male headteachers in junior and primary schools are 'normal'.

'Discrimination [against women] does occur in relation to teacher employment' (EOC, 1985). Feminists argue that we live in a patriarchal society in which men assume the positions of power and responsibility. Discrimination is rooted in traditional assumptions that are taken for granted, and in stereotypes of men and women's capabilities, strengths and weaknesses, and of the roles and attitudes which are appropriate for them. Some men and some women are trapped by their own socialization and many are trapped by the perceptions and opinions of other people. We have come a long way from the climate in which the President of the NAS felt able to publicly say that 'only a nation heading for a madhouse would force upon men – many married with families – such a position as service under a spinster headmistress' (*Woman Teacher*, 1939). However, the fact that by the end of the 1980s women were less well represented in senior positions than they were at the start of the decade (DES, 1989a) shows that there is still a great distance to travel before women teachers come to enjoy anything like equal career experiences and opportunities to those of men. The following letter, from the *Times Educational Supplement* of 14 December 1990, makes this very clear:

> When the headship of my village primary school became vacant, the chair of the governors announced at the annual parish meeting that the school would be appointing a new headmaster. When questioned from the floor whether a prerequisite for the job was to be male he answered in the affirmative and added that if a man and woman of equal ability presented themselves he would choose the man.

WOMEN TEACHERS' EXPERIENCES IN SCHOOL

Schools are part of society and are, therefore, subject to prevalent social attitudes. As is the case among the population at large, individual teachers have sexist attitudes and beliefs. Sara Delamont (1990) suggests that the working- and lower-middle-class backgrounds of many teachers mean that they are especially likely to hold traditional gender role stereotypes. However, while the beliefs and attitudes held by individuals can be influential, the general ethos and the institutional and organizational practices and customs of schools also have considerable impact on how teachers as well as pupils experience being female or male at school.

As we have seen, there are fewer women in senior positions. Consequently women lack formal power and have limited opportunity to influence official policy- and decision-making. This means that, within schools, teachers' and students' experiences are generally determined by men and by male values. In addition, the preponderance of men in senior posts results in a dearth of female role models. There are few examples of 'successful' women in schools; therefore traditional stereotypes are not challenged and the 'normalness' of male authority is reinforced, which has depressing implications for female aspirations. It also means that children see few women in senior positions. This bodes ill for the future because 'even young children are capable of assimilating and internalizing role stereotypes where authority, power and status is invested in the male' (Marsh, 1990, p. 19).

Research suggests that senior male managers tend to prefer 'authoritarian' forms of management (Al-Khalifa, 1989). In recent years there has been a strong trend towards applying the principles and practices of industrial and commercial management to schools. This trend has been reinforced by the Education Reform Act (1988) with its emphasis on market forces, parental/consumer choice and local management of schools. Feminists have argued that many of these principles and practices are closely linked to values and attitudes which are traditionally associated with masculinity. Management involves 'aggressive competitive behaviours, emphasis on control rather than negotiation and collaboration, and the pursuit of competition rather than shared problem solving' (Al-Khalifa, 1989, p. 89). Elizabeth Al-Khalifa suggests that some women feel these are 'repugnant and dysfunctional' (*ibid.*). Hence women tend to avoid applying for jobs in which they believe they would be required to practice such behaviours.

Interestingly, concern about the effects 'masculine' authority has on school ethos has led some schools to experiment with more collaborative and personal types of approach; approaches more in tune with what are regarded as 'feminine' characteristics. Indeed, research in American schools has revealed that 'achievement in reading and maths is higher, . . . there is less violence and . . . staff and student morale is higher' (Shakeshaft, 1986, p. 153) when women occupy the senior management posts. But this is unusual. As Caroline Benn writes,

> Historically, there have always been two distinct teaching functions: the first an extension of mothering, and reserved for women; the second an extension of power and authority, reserved for men, who have guarded it well. This division – while no longer explicit – is still important throughout the education system. (Benn, 1989, p. xix)

Aspinwall and Drummond (1989) suggest that, in the main, the expectation is that women teachers will be found working in 'traditional', 'feminine' areas. Thus it is seen as 'natural' for women to work with young children and to adopt the caring 'mother/teacher' role (see also Steedman, 1982; H. Burgess, 1989). Conversely male teachers in infant schools are often viewed with suspicion and their sexual orientation may well be called into question.

In the secondary school, when it comes to the allocation of tasks and responsibilities, even at deputy head level, gender related boundaries have tended to be clearly evident. This has led to what more than one woman deputy has described as the 'tea, Tampax, and flowers' job (Davidson, 1985, p. 194; R. Grant, 1987). In other words woman deputy heads are often expected to deal with pastoral matters, in particular what are often referred to as 'girls' problems', and to take charge of providing refreshments for visitors to the school, whereas their male counterparts have responsibility for the timetable, 'discipline' and curriculum and staff development. It is also interesting to note that, given stereotypical expectations, women teachers are frequently expected to do more work for less money or to accept lower gradings for similar work (Weightman, 1989).

Advertising and recruitment of teachers

The Sex Discrimination Act (1975) stated that

> When advertising job vacancies, [it is an offence] . . . to publish or cause to be published an advertisement which indicates or might reasonably be understood as indicating an intention to discriminate unlawfully on grounds of sex or marriage.

Consequently, in its guidelines relating to teacher employment the EOC suggested that

> Use of a job description with a sexist connotation (such as 'Headmaster') must be avoided. Even phrases such as 'vacancy due to retirement of present headmaster' may give the impression that applications are invited from persons of one sex only (EOC, 1985, p. 9)

and, with regard to senior jobs, that

> It is all too easy for part of a job description to give the impression that applications will not be welcomed from persons of one sex even though such persons have the skills and experience for a management post. (*ibid.*)

117

Unfortunately these guidelines are not always adhered to. For example, on 28 September 1990 the *Times Educational Supplement* carried this advertisement:

URGENT APPOINTMENT – Deputy Headteacher

Although [X] is a boys' school, it has developed a non-traditional approach. The ethos is positive with high value placed on non-aggression, mutual support and good relationships between pupils and staff.

The Governors are looking for an enthusiastic and dynamic deputy head-master who will both meet the organisational and managerial challenges of the 1990s and inspire the continuing development of quality teaching and learning.

And there are still advertisements for senior jobs in primary schools which refer to interest, experience or ability in teaching 'boys' football' (see EOC, 1985, p. 25).

Sexual harassment

So far we have focused on women's experiences as they are reflected in the formal career and management arena. There is, of course, another, informal, but no less significant side which concerns how women are regarded and treated as women in schools:

Sexual harassment has been considered normal behaviour in the relationship between men and women at work throughout history: (Sedley and Benn, 1982, p. 5)

R. Burgess (1989) quoted a woman teacher who said that sexist comments were 'something you learn to live with'. Indeed the research which does exist (for example, Woods, 1979; Ball, 1987; R. Burgess, 1989; Cunnison, 1989; DeLyon, 1989) suggests that sexual joking and innuendo are commonplace and taken for granted in many staffrooms. This can range from 'soft' ribbing, in the form of comments about dizzy blondes or references to 'my harem' by the male primary school head of a female staff, to 'harder' and more obviously offensive personal remarks about a woman's sexual behaviour. One of the writers of this book knows of a boys' school with a predominantly male staff where at the end of each term a 'Golden Cock' award is presented to the man deemed to have 'bedded' the most women. One year a new woman teacher was so honoured because she was believed to be promiscuous and 'a slag'. The male headteacher did not see fit to take any action following the woman's complaint.

There is also outright sexual harassment, from male colleagues and from pupils – even from very young children (see Walkerdine, 1981: we have discussed sexual harassment of pupils in Chapter 6). This can vary from comments to actual physical assault. Women teachers, like other women workers, often find themselves in a difficult position when they experience such harassment (see Whitbread, 1988). When the perpetrator is a senior member of staff, they may be afraid to complain in case they jeopardize their career prospects. Radical feminists have drawn our attention to the meaning of sexual harassment. Their view is that sexual harassment is about power and about putting women down. This means that some men may engage in it because they perceive women as threats to their career progress (Cunnison, 1989, pp. 59–60).

Not all schools treat sexual harassment by and of staff or pupils seriously, not least because it is not unusual for such behaviour to be seen as 'natural' and 'normal' for men and something which women should learn to put up with. Following this understanding it is not surprising to find that lesbian and gay teachers can have an extremely difficult time in school (see, for example, Gill, 1989; Jones and Mahony, 1989; Squirrell, 1989).

GENDER IN INITIAL TEACHER EDUCATION (ITE)

Although certain critics (such as Sheila Lawlor and Anthony O'Hear) view the introduction of gender issues into teacher education as 'faddish concerns' of 'loony leftists' (Lawlor, 1990), it is officially required by the various agencies responsible for validating and monitoring initial teacher education that they should (at least) be raised. The Council for the Accreditation of Teacher Education asks that courses make students aware of the Sex Discrimination Act (1975) and of the need to teach in ways that do not discriminate against children on grounds of gender or 'race'; while the DES state that students should 'guard against preconceptions based on the . . . sex of pupils (DES, 1984, p. 11), and 'on completion of their course . . . should be . . . able to incorporate in their teaching cross-curricular dimensions (e.g. equal opportunities)' (DES, 1989c, p. 10, 6.2).

As a result of their own socialization and experiences it is not surprising that research shows that many student teachers hold 'deeply entrenched and pernicious . . . sexually differentiated educational expectations for girls and boys' (Spender and Sarah, 1982, p. 138; see also Skelton and Hanson, 1989). An investigation involving 155 first-year students on a BA with Qualified Teacher Status course found that over 25 per cent of them expected boys, but not girls, to be reckless, untidy, cheeky, brave, noisy and naughty; and expected girls, but not boys, to be tidy, clean, quiet, sensible, obedient, passive and well-behaved (Sikes, 1991). Such findings are disturbing if, as seems likely,

where teachers hold such expectations about the interests, abilities, conduct and personalities of their male and female pupils . . . they may, by the encouragement they give and the stimuli they provide, heighten any such differences as may exist and create special problems for the boy or girl who does not conform to type. (Stanworth, 1981, p. 21)

Clearly, if equal opportunities are the aim, student teachers need to be helped to address the gender-related expectations and assumptions that they themselves take for granted. Unfortunately, the evidence (Skelton, 1985, 1987, 1989) suggests that some ITE courses actually reinforce gender differentiation through their hidden curriculum. This is, perhaps, partly because there are no detailed official guidelines on what is to be covered under the heading of gender or on how it is to be approached. In some colleges equal opportunities issues are tacked on to existing courses. One or two lectures deal with equal opportunities as a matter separate from the 'mainstream' course content. It may be that this kind of 'token' approach does more harm than good. Another approach is to offer equal opportunities material as an optional or extra course. This means that it is not presented as an area which is of significance for all students.

Other departments have tried to permeate the whole curriculum with the issue, or have run specific, compulsory courses on gender and 'race' issues. It is difficult to know which is the ideal approach because very little research has been done into the matter. J. Hanson (1987) feels that permeation is the most effective method but points out that it is important to monitor the implementation of such initiatives to ensure that they actually do address the issues – not least because there is evidence to suggest that some tutors involved in initial teacher education are hostile to the gender issue (Thompson, 1989).

It does seem that it is not enough to treat gender issues as a separate topic, simply because differentiation and discrimination permeate all aspects of life. They certainly permeate what goes on in schools and this is why even students who hold egalitarian views and who are committed to equal opportunities may find that once they get into schools and classrooms the practical exigencies of survival may seem to be best tackled by strategies which contradict and conflict with their personal beliefs (Hanson and Herrington, 1976; Clarricoates, 1980a, 1980b; Whyte, 1983b; Sikes, Measor and Woods, 1985; Acker, 1988; Menter, 1989).

GENDER IN IN-SERVICE TEACHER EDUCATION

In-service work with practising teachers is also important (Orr, 1985; Taylor, 1985). Some teachers are interested in the equal opportunities issue, but it is important to emphasize that there can be considerable resistance, and many writers have discussed the difficulties they have faced when trying to implement change in the area. It is perhaps unreasonable to expect teachers to change their approach or their classroom practice overnight without some in-service work and advice. The responsibility of in-service training is, therefore, 'to provide teachers with sufficient understanding to make professional sense of the demands for change being made upon them and sufficient support to enable them to step beyond understanding into action in their schools' (Taylor, 1985, pp. 105–6).

The strategies that LEAs have used include the following:

1 Running in-service days with innovative workshops and projects (Thompson, 1989; Sheffield LAPP team, 1990).
2 Appointing advisory teachers with responsibility for equal opportunities work.
3 Developing resource centres.
4 Establishing support groups for interested teachers.
5 Funding secondments and research posts.

There is controversy over what are the most effective strategies for in-service work in equal opportunities, but we have detailed accounts of a number of effective in-service projects, which show the impact that carefully planned and well-resourced programmes can have. Rochdale and Tameside, for example, adopted a 'power-based' model of change and used a top-down approach in their TVEI Related In-Service Training-funded work. They were determined that gender equality should have central role. Training was given first of all to education officers, advisers and headteachers; in the second stage the focus was on deputy heads; and finally on middle management and classroom teachers. Other schemes have taken different approaches. The SCDC/EOC 'Genderwatch' scheme, for example, did not aim to start by influencing senior management and concentrated on work with teachers. This was more of a 'bottom-up' approach.

It is clear that both approaches have something to recommend them. Above all, however, it is important to foster a sense of 'ownership' of any initiative for change in schools because this promotes commitment.

CONCLUSIONS AND ASSESSMENT

Attention to equal opportunities in initial and in-service teacher education varies tremendously from institution to institution and from LEA to LEA. Much depends upon the enthusiasm and commitment of key individuals. There are also financial and political implications. Equal opportunities is a controversial area and support for initiatives and policies depends to some extent upon who holds the power. For example, we know of one northern LEA which, throughout the 1970s and 1980s, built up impressive support services for equal opportunities work. A change in the balance of power in the council meant swingeing cuts because equal opportunities were no longer seen as important, let alone a priority.

CHAPTER OVERVIEW

In this chapter we have seen that women are dramatically under-represented in senior positions and that even in primary schools, where the majority of teachers are women, men occupy a greater number of headships. A number of reasons have been put forward to explain this discrepancy but evidence suggests that assumptions about women's commitment, persistence and ambition are, to a large extent, myths. In schools, as in society at large, women are discriminated against, are channelled into stereotypical jobs and experience sexual harassment.

Since those in charge of schools are usually men, management tends to be male-oriented and male-dominated. This may have negative implications for pupil achievement as well as for women teachers' experience.

Attention to gender issues is among the requirements for the accreditation of initial teacher education courses. However, the extent to which gender issues are tackled varies considerably. As a result of their socialization, student teachers may hold differential expectations for boys and girls. If progress is to be made and equality advanced, gender needs to occupy a prominent place in initial and in-service teacher education.

SUGGESTIONS FOR FURTHER READING

Acker, S. (ed.) (1989) *Teachers, Gender and Careers*. Basingstoke: Falmer.

De Lyon, H. and Widdowson Migniuolo, F. (eds) (1989) *Women Teachers: Issues and Experiences*. Milton Keynes: Open University Press.

Both of these books contain a collection of interesting chapters about various aspects of women teachers' experiences in school.

CHAPTER 8

Ways forward

CHAPTER SUMMARY

In this chapter we look at some of the strategies that have been implemented to remedy the problems of gender inequality in schools. We first deal with the controversies that surround the issue and the discussions about the most effective approach. We then focus on the issues of school organization, the curriculum, assessment and careers advice, which we have identified as being important in earlier chapters. The chapter ends with an assessment of the schemes that have been tried out and offers some suggestions for the future.

So far in this book we have tried to show how schools function to create and reinforce gender differences and inequalities. In this chapter we will focus on what has been done to try and solve some of these problems. As the issue of gender inequality came to the attention of teachers and education policy-makers, they began to experiment with ways of improving the situation in schools. We will look at some of these initiatives and at the different policies that have been tried out. We will aim to offer some critical assessment of their respective advantages and effectiveness. The chapter is divided into four sections:

1 Controversies. There are a number of different approaches to tackling gender inequalities in schools. We look at the differences in theories and practice between them.
2 Programmes to implement change. There are national initiatives, local education authority schemes and projects implemented by individual schools and individual teachers.

3 Problems with what has already been done. There are both practical and theoretical problems with schemes that have been implemented.
4 Ways forward in the future.

CONTROVERSIES

Equal opportunities work is controversial in schools. Not all those involved in running or consuming education approve of tackling the matter, and even among those who are committed to work in the field of gender stereotyping there are disagreements. A number of different approaches to the eradication of gender inequality in schooling have developed. They connect with the factions in feminist theory that we outlined in Chapter 2. It is possible to divide the approaches into 'liberal' and 'radical' models (Mason and Jewson, 1986).

Liberal models

The liberal model is concerned to establish equality of opportunity. It aims to use positive action to create a system where all individuals are able to compete freely and equally for success and rewards, in school or in the wider society. The policy-maker acts as a kind of umpire or referee, who makes sure that the mechanisms which select people are fair and just. This means that equal opportunities policies need to set up fair procedures and to make sure that both direct and indirect forms of discrimination are avoided.

Criticisms of this approach

The 'radical' view is that there are pupils who begin school with profound disadvantages and who therefore cannot compete on an equal footing. These individuals and groups need special provision and extra help if they are to develop their potential. Positive discrimination strategies are necessary. This means that it is not enough to treat pupils in a standardized way in school, for standard treatment does not mean equal treatment. Many writers have been critical of the liberal approach, whether it is applied in relation to class, gender or 'race'. They make the point that pupils need to be recognized as members of significantly different social groups. Different groups have different problems and needs.

Radical models

The radical models seek to intervene in schools in order to achieve a fair distribution of rewards among those who are members of disadvantaged groups. They are concerned with the outcomes of the contest, with who wins in the system, rather than with the rules of the game. Positive discrimination is used to advance the interests of the groups that are oppressed and disadvantaged.

Fonda developed a model of these different approaches, which hopefully makes the differences clear:

- The Unlocked Door: All options are open to both boys and girls, but there is no recognition of gender bias in curriculum, lesson content, teaching method and assessment.
- The Open Door: Options have been screened to ensure that neither sex is deterred from choosing them, and no student is rejected because of gender.
- The Special Escalator: Affirmative strategies are used to provide key opportunities for either boys or girls.
- Equal Outcomes: Provision is radically restructured to secure equal take-up, qualifications and achievements among boys and girls. (NFER, 1989)

When the last two approaches have been employed, they have produced controversy. The criticism is that positive discrimination strategies are inherently discriminatory. There has also been concern that they will lead to a lowering of standards overall, as equal competition supposedly selects the best candidates.

In the context of education and gender, two basic models have developed, one liberal and one radical.

Equal opportunities approach: a liberal model

In the equal opportunities perspective, the concern is with achieving equal access for girls to existing educational resources. Girls should have full rights to all areas of the curriculum and school facilities, and any classroom or feature of school organization which disadvantages them should be removed. 'Equal access to the SAME CURRICULUM is essential including equal access to additional subjects not included in the core or foundation curriculum' (EOC, 1987). The principle is that girls should get equal shares of the cake as it exists (Skelton, 1989).

Anti-sexist approach: a radical model

The second perspective is the radical anti-sexist one. Here the demand is for a new and different educational cake, and for the development of new school structures and curricula which are 'girl-friendly'. Equal access to the curriculum and resources is not enough: 'We have learned from two decades of research that an essential pre-requisite is to re-select and organise the forms of educational knowledge transmitted' (Arnot, 1989, p. 7).

A common curriculum is a necessary but not a sufficient condition to break down educational inequalities. The problem is that much of the curriculum that we now have simply 'reaffirms male priorities' (Kant, 1987). 'Female subjects', such as domestic science and child-care, have low status in our schools. By contrast the curriculum spheres in which boys excel and the teachers are predominantly male have high status. The anti-sexist approach emphasizes the importance of male–female power relationships and of the ways that these may disadvantage girls in school. Those who adopt an anti-sexist approach suggest that the equal opportunity approach fails to deal with this patriarchal element to gender inequalities, because it fails to acknowledge the vested interests of those who have power and who will hold on to that power. 'It assumes that change will come about through consensus without conflict' (Lees and Scott, 1990, p. 335). Lees argues for an acknowledgement that change involves conflict and that conflict can be progressive (Walkerdine also discusses this issue, 1984).

The existence of two approaches in the area of sexism in education is paralleled in race work by the existence of the multicultural perspective and the anti-racist one. In theory liberal feminists tend to adopt equal opportunity models, while socialist and radical feminists support the anti-sexist approaches. However, both models of intervention share some areas of concern, interest and activity, and their proponents can learn from each other, despite their fundamental differences.

Nevertheless, the kind of policy that individual local education authorities or teachers adopt will reflect the kind of theoretical understanding that they have about the causes of gender inequality in society. The great majority of gender initiatives that have been launched or backed by official agencies, central government or LEAs, for example, have specifically had the equal opportunities perspective.

Conclusion

In conclusion we can say that work on gender inequality in schools remains controversial, and central government has taken what observers have called a 'neutral stance'. There is no general agreement about strategies for change among those who are convinced of its importance. This is probably inevitable, given the highly political nature of the problems involved, and the essential conflict over values and ways of life that it implies. It is also true that the work is still fairly new and it is perhaps right that a good deal of trial and error should take place.

PROGRAMMES TO IMPLEMENT CHANGE

In this section we look at the different strategies that have been tried out at national and local level to implement equal opportunities. In the chapters on the primary and secondary schools we listed the factors that had been identified as important, and we can combine those lists as follows:

1 The organization of the school
2 Curriculum and content of lessons
3 The hidden curriculum and teachers' attitudes and expectations
4 External examinations and assessment
5 The world of work and careers advice

These are the issues which have by and large been tackled by the equal opportunity programmes, and we will deal with them in turn. Initial teacher training schemes and in-service courses have aimed to deal with the questions of teachers' attitudes and expectations, and they have been covered in Chapter 7.

The organization of the school

Many schools and local authorities have adopted the strategy of equal opportunity policies to change the sex-segregation practices in schools. This has not been general across the UK; some LEAs have agreed and written equal opportunity policies for all the schools in their areas while others have not tackled this at all or left it up to individual schools. The levels of resourcing and commitment to equal opportunities policies varies considerably between LEAs (Burchell and Millman, 1989).

We include examples of equal opportunities policies from nursery, primary and secondary schools in Appendix 2. There are some common features that we can identify. The policies emphasize the significance of looking at 'very mundane school routine as a basis for building a foundation for work to promote equality' (Burchell and Millman, 1989, p. 15). Issues like changing registers to an alphabetical format and making school uniform unisex are important. School routines have been changed to encourage all children to take equal responsibility for a wide range of matters, whether carrying chairs or the care of new children in the school.

The playground

One key element in the equal opportunity policies has been change in the way playgrounds are run and monitored by teachers. Horniman School in London ran a successful scheme, as follows:

1 They restricted the area in which the boys were allowed to play football.
2 They opened up the school hall as a quiet area.
3 They introduced a number of co-operative games in the playground.
4 They banned expensive electronic toys, guns, swords and sweets.

The policies were welcomed by the quieter boys as well as by the girls (ILEA, 1987, has more examples of schemes, and we include a list of resources in Appendix 1).

Assemblies

> Assemblies involve a shared experience, have high status in children's eyes and can have considerable impact. Assembly presents the public face – what the school stands for. (ILEA, 1987, p. 20)

Schools have introduced equal opportunity themes and focused on gender issues in their assemblies. Latchmere School ran 'her-story' assemblies based on history projects; another class used their project on sexism in reading schemes. We include a list of resources for making equal opportunity points in assembly organization in Appendix 1.

School equal opportunity policies: an assessment

There is controversy over the effectiveness of whole-school equal opportunities policies. The argument is the same as the one applied to national legislation: it is important to have policies in place, but on their own they can have only limited effect. The existence of a policy is no guarantee, but the absence of such policies makes it less likely that committed practitioners will be taken seriously (NFER, 1989).

Lees and Scott in recent research (1990) have questioned the value of equal opportunities policies, arguing that they have only limited impact on the power structures and day-to-day running of institutions. Lees and Scott press for continuous monitoring to ensure implementation, pointing out that the monitoring needs to be done by those with some authority so that there is some 'top-down' support.

Curriculum and content of lessons

Many equal opportunity initiatives have taken the curriculum as the focus of their work. We need to look at national initiatives, at local schemes but also at the work of individual teachers and schools, in which every area of the school curriculum has been scrutinized for discriminatory practices. It is important that the work of individuals and small groups is not lost sight of in the midst of the national initiatives, because it often takes a more radical stance and can in some ways be a pace-setter for wider official schemes.

National schemes

There are a number of nation-wide initiatives which have aimed to intervene in the curriculum to improve equal opportunities. Most of these have been directed at secondary schools. The Education Reform Act has implications for gender inequalities, and TVEI and the science projects like GAST and GIST are also significant.

The National Curriculum

Feminists have made a number of criticisms of the equal opportunity implications of the Education Reform Act (1988). We will list them for the sake of clarity:

1 Substantial in-service training will be necessary if the provisions of the National Curriculum are to be carried out.
2 There is already a shortage of good, well-qualified teachers of maths, physics and technology. The National Curriculum will make this shortfall more serious, and steps must be taken to deal with the problem and to ensure that there are women teachers of these subjects available.
3 The National Curriculum has chosen to emphasize particular kinds of knowledge. Those who support an anti-sexist approach suggest that it reinforces all of the traditional and male-dominated areas of knowledge.
4 There is not enough acknowledgement in the documents of the differences in performance between boys and girls in particular curriculum areas. There is a need for remedial or booster courses to be developed if all pupils are to meet the attainment targets.
5 The National Curriculum fails to acknowledge that there are gender differences in learning styles, or to offer much scope for experimentation with alternative provision, like single-sex setting, for example.
6 All new curriculum materials and assessment materials should be gender neutral and must be conscious of the need to eliminate sex bias.
7 There is no concern for gender equality in the assessment structures that have been established so far. We know that some strategies disadvantage girls.
8 Resources need to be made available to provide adequate science and technology facilities in single-sex girls' schools.

9 The National Curriculum has not tackled the problem of the hidden curriculum, where traditional assumptions and discriminating practices still exist.

10 There was no priority given to the placing of adequate numbers of women and members of ethnic minorities on the working parties of the National Curriculum Council.

It is too soon to make a final judgement on the educational reforms, as schools are still engaged in implementing the National Curriculum, but criticism of its weaknesses has not faded. It remains to be seen whether in the long term the problems connected with equal opportunities provision can be solved.

TVEI and other science-oriented schemes

TVEI schemes had two main equal opportunity objectives: to ensure that girls and boys joined the scheme in roughly equal numbers and to encourage pupils on the scheme to make non-traditional choices. The NFER evaluated TVEI and concluded that the project had found it difficult to implement its equal opportunities commitments (NFER, 1989). More boys than girls joined the scheme in their fourth year at school; the boys on the scheme took the technological, engineering and electronics options, and the girls by and large took the caring and catering subjects. However, TVEI schools and colleges had a better record on encouraging girls into non-traditional subject areas than schools outside the scheme. In addition, TVEI schools could claim a breakthrough in one curriculum area, as they were successful in persuading girls to take information technology (Table 8.1).

Table 8.1 Summary of TVEI intakes by sex, 1983–6

Year	Boys		Girls	
	Number	%	Number	%
1983	2203	54.7	1822	45.3
1984	9653	58.5	6854	41.5
1985	11262	57.0	8512	43.0
1986	14033	55.1	11449	44.9

Source: Manpower Services Commission, TVEI Unit.

The figures in Table 8.1, however, date from a time before TVEI was extended to operate in all secondary schools. The high levels of funding that characterized the early schemes have disappeared and there is some uncertainty as to whether these figures can be maintained, or indeed whether the equal opportunities criteria will remain in place.

A number of general principles have emerged as a result of monitoring TVEI. First, it is clear that TVEI schemes which were run in schools and an LEA that have a well-worked-out equal opportunities policy have been able to achieve the most change. The second principle is that support, guidance and counselling are needed throughout all stages of the scheme. If pupils are persuaded to make a non-traditional subject choice, then they need help in the classroom and also on their work placement. 'Role play, mock interviews, profiling and counselling can provide valuable support for students following non-traditional courses' (NFER, 1989, p. 34). Non-traditional work placements require that the employer is well prepared for the issues which may arise for the young person, and the pupil is also well prepared and supported throughout.

GIST, GATE, WISE and other science-based approaches

In Chapter 3 we introduced the initiatives and the projects specifically directed to improving girls' attitudes and motivation toward the science areas of the curriculum. GIST and GATE are the best known, although there are others like WISE, (Women into Science and Engineering). Here the EOC funded a bus which was fitted out with a workshop and equipped with people able to give career advice on the sciences. The bus visits schools at their request. Another important strategy was the VISTA programme: this brought women scientists into schools to talk about an aspect of their job which was already covered by the school science syllabus.

The projects have drawn teachers' attention to the ways science is taught in schools, and emphasized the importance of making school science more 'girl-friendly'; that is, 'a science which will appeal equally to the interests and concerns of girls and boys' (Whyte, 1985). The initiatives suggested that girls were interested in the social implications of science and also nature, the environment and medical science. GIST found that boys were equally interested in these areas. Girls were not interested in home-based and domestic matters. As a result the schemes could recommend that schools develop curricula and lesson material which build on the shared interests of boys and girls.

The science schemes also worked on 'girl-friendly' methods of teaching. It is becoming clear that the research brief that teachers set is important. Grant (1983) suggests that research problems which have relevance to real human contexts engage girls' interests. He considered that this was equally important to searching for 'girl-friendly' topics.

Science schemes: an assessment

In the 'action' schools (where GIST interventions took place), the attitudes of children became noticeably more liberal, especially on sex role and occupational stereotypes and the 'masculinity' of science. However, the GIST project team found that changing attitudes was not enough to ensure that pupils' option choices changed at GCSE. The problem is an intractable one. In Chapter 5 we discussed the radical and socialist feminist criticisms of the science intervention schemes. They argued that the schemes have a 'liberal' orientation, and do not go far enough to produce significant change.

There have been a number of nation-wide initiatives which have included equal opportunity principles. The Educational Reform Act (1988) has many implications for the processes of gender stereotyping in schools. New schemes like TVEI have also alerted schools, colleges and local authorities to the importance of equal opportunities. Science initiatives draw attention to the need to develop 'girl-friendly' teaching strategies.

School-based and individual teacher strategies

Whatever the effects of these large-scale interventions are in Britain, much of the work that has promoted equal opportunities in the curriculum has been launched by individual schools and individual teachers. In this section we will describe this work, indicating the sorts of strategy which have been employed across the curriculum, as space prevents us from dealing with all curriculum areas individually. There is a list of resources for different subject areas and further information in Appendix 1.

Access to the curriculum: classroom strategies

Access to the curriculum is a central issue in equal opportunities work, but writers who take the anti-sexist approach do not feel that equal access is enough. They emphasize the quality of pupils' experience of the curriculum at the classroom level (Egan, 1990). Individual teachers and schools have tried to develop strategies which can help remedy the curriculum imbalance that we discussed in Chapters 4 and 5.

Teachers have experimented with a number of strategies to improve children's skills in all areas of the curriculum. The early years are seen to be important. In nursery schools, teachers have spent time with girls on activities which they perhaps do not normally choose (Hodgeon, 1988). Hodgeon discusses the importance of the female teacher showing confidence and competence when dealing with tools and equipment which are perhaps usually thought of as 'male'.

Teachers have also ensured that girls get equal access to the large out-door toys which boys often monopolize.

In primary schools, teachers have reorganized the 'home corner', replacing the wendy house with resources for all children to play out a range of imaginative games. Themes like the bank, the café, the post office and the optician or the dentist have been popular. If boys avoided the wendy house because it seemed to belong to the girls, they missed out on a range of important play experiences. The intention is to open the range of activities for all children.

In curriculum areas which have been defined as belonging to boys, teachers have intervened. They have logged the amount of time that boys spend on the computer or technical equipment as opposed to girls, and have used the information to enforce more equal access (Culley, 1986). Other schools have offered girls the opportunity to develop confidence in areas like CDT by giving girls experience in building models in single-sex groups initially, or running girls'-only clubs in information technology (EOC/London Borough of Croydon, 1985). Approaching technological and scientific subjects through drama and art work seems to be able to help girls to engage with them. Teachers also assert the importance of offering praise and encouragement to girls when they experiment with unfamiliar curriculum areas.

Single-sex setting

Another strategy that has been tried out by some schools is single-sex setting. Pupils are taught in single-sex groups for some subjects, usually the sciences, maths and CDT. One of the best-known examples is Stamford High School, which adopted a policy of single-sex sets for the teaching of mathematics (S. Smith, 1987). When pupils in this mixed school were taught in single-sex classes for some years, girls' performance, as measured by examination results, improved. The best results were achieved by offering segregated setting for maths in the early years of secondary school. It is possible that factors other than the single-sex setting were significant in achieving this result – attending a school in which teachers were committed to girls' mathematical performance may be crucial – nevertheless, the school concluded that single-sex setting in the early years was well worth trying.

Assessment of these strategies

A number of TVEI schemes are currently experimenting with single-sex teaching for technical subjects, and their results should enable us to develop a better assessment of the effectiveness of the strategy. It is worth pointing out that some teachers have been opposed to this strategy, on the grounds that it forms a kind of discrimination in itself and also that it only postpones difficulties that pupils will meet later in life. It is clear that single-sex setting needs to be located in the context of a whole-school policy of equal opportunities for girls if it is to work efficiently.

Textbooks

Feminist research has argued that sex-stereotyping in school textbooks has a negative influence on children. There is more gender neutral material available now than in the past, but clearly it is not always possible to replace textbooks, given the resources crisis which affects British schools at this time. Not all new material promotes equal opportunities; some publishers are more aware of its significance than others. The Croydon project on equal opportunities in information technology had worked on a resource book on IT for schools, and had searched at length for a photograph which showed a woman in charge of a complicated piece of technological equipment. When the book was published, the publisher had substituted a picture showing a man (EOC/London Borough of Croydon, 1985, p. 20).

Feminist groups have argued that commercial organizations and pressures cannot be allowed to dictate the content of textbooks. In Britain there is little government support for equal opportunity principles, in contrast with Germany, for example, where textbooks cannot be licensed unless they promote co-education and limit bias in sex roles (Weiner, 1990, p. 190). Many organizations exist, however, which filter British textbooks and recommend those which have shown a commitment to gender equality (see Appendix 1).

Individual teachers have developed strategies for working with sex-stereotyped books which are in schools. In some schools pupils are encouraged to identify gender bias in the books and to develop critical appraisal skills in their reading. When faced with a lack of appropriate material, teachers have developed their own. Payne (1980) describes producing a booklet on women's history. Her class concentrated on discovering the history of their local community and the role that women had played in it. She found that other schools wanted to use the booklet, and they had to reprint it. Other teachers used a specifically oral history approach; one Northumberland school had the grandmothers of its children coming into school to tell about their experience of the world wars, and a project developed from that (Windass, 1989).

Children's stories and literature

Feminist teachers have also focused on the problems presented by children's story books, since it is not only textbooks that portray stereotyped images of women. Many anti-sexist stories and books have been written and produced, some of which we described in Chapter 4. Titles like *Polly the Wrestling Princess* and *Mrs Plug the Plumber* give a clear picture of the author's intent. However, it must be acknowledged that this can be a controversial area. While some of the stories are without doubt exciting and appropriate for use with children, some teachers find they are stilted and artificial, and do not have the merits of older stories and writing. A number of organizations provide lists of anti-sexist fiction, and we include a list of them in Appendix 1.

Teachers in some schools have used the older stories but asked children to engage with the stories critically, to look at the gender stereotyping within them, and to produce their own stories with different themes. Similar strategies have been employed with reading schemes. In one project pupils analysed reading schemes in their school for bias. The Genderwatch scheme offers a checklist which can be used to make a quick analysis of books, reading schemes and worksheets to ascertain their bias (Whyte, 1983a; Myers, 1987).

Display work

Teachers have identified displays as an important equal opportunities resource. Displays can provide a range of positive images of women. There are particularly good resources produced in the science and technology areas: ILEA, for example, produced posters as part of their *Women in Engineering* pack. The Engineering Industry Training Board have also produced a range of illustrated material showing women in non-traditional careers. We provide a list of resources in Appendix 1.

One favoured strategy has been to make displays of women's art, books and drama work and of women in history. One teacher ran a project in which pupils had collected newspaper, magazine and advertisement material which indicated the media portrayal of women. 'They were mounted in an enormous collage on a classroom wall' (Windass, 1989, p. 45). Other teachers have made a point of providing displays where female heroes from the children's own locality are featured.

Projects on equal opportunity themes

Teachers have attempted to change bias in established areas of the curriculum, and they have also tried to introduce the study of equal opportunity issues into the classroom. Pupils have worked on projects which look critically at the images of women in advertising, in newspapers and on television. We have accounts of teachers encouraging pupils to analyse the romance magazines and love-story comics that are produced for girls. (Payne, 1980). Parents and the local community have been invited into schools to provide 'living' examples of equal opportunity issues. Many schools have run topics on 'mums', showing the range of work they did in both community and home and inviting women with non-stereotyped jobs and hobbies into the school.

Drama and art work have the potential to highlight equal opportunities issues. For instance, in drama lessons in one school children acted out a play about a planet where women had all the power. They took on non-stereotyped roles to enable them to try them out. When the girls presented this play at assembly the boys became very defensive about the criticism they were hearing. A formal debate was held and the motion that boys and girls can work together co-operatively was carried. A book has been published which gives suggestions for project work in the primary school on equal opportunities issues (Antonouris and Wilson, 1989).

Individual strategies: an assessment

It is clearly difficult to assess the effectiveness of individual work which originates from committed teachers. It is important for the children in their care and for the schools they work in. However, there is inevitably a limit to what the individual teacher can achieve, and it is easy for that individual to feel overwhelmed by the extent of the problem. It is clear that teachers working in schools where there is support from the senior management teams and from the LEA have a greater chance of success.

Conclusions

Many equal opportunity schemes have chosen to focus on the curriculum. We have looked in some detail at these to give a flavour of their work. The curriculum clearly has a central role in the processes by which schools reinforce sex role learning and direct pupils along particular career paths. National and local initiatives have aimed to help correct the curriculum imbalances that exist, with girls and boys choosing very different subject areas. Nevertheless, the problem remains difficult to solve. Individual schools have experimented with single-sex setting for some subjects, and this strategy is presently being tested more widely. Teachers at all levels of the school system have aimed to teach in ways that are free from prejudice, and which enable children to identify the bias and discriminatory practices of schools and other institutions in society.

The hidden curriculum and teacher attitudes and expectations

Equal opportunity and anti-sexist initiatives on the hidden curriculum have concentrated on attempting to alert teachers to the part they themselves play in gender socialization. The aim has been to make teachers aware of their own attitudes and of the discriminatory effects of some of their practices.

At a local level, in-service courses have been an important strategy and some schools and LEAs have written clauses on the hidden curriculum into their equal opportunity policies. Others have appointed advisory teachers with responsibility for equal opportunities; ILEA developed this policy, for example (Taylor, 1985). Other strategies include developing resource banks of bias-free material and establishing working parties and local networks. (We have outlined in-service provision for equal opportunities issues in Chapter 7, and more details of the work can be found there.) Local authority support makes it clear to those who teach in and run its schools that equal opportunities are an important issue in the authority, and are to be taken seriously (Fawcett Society, 1988). If a climate can be created in which gender issues are taken seriously then discriminatory practices are more likely to change at classroom level.

Individual teachers have also developed their own strategies and it is these we must turn to next.

Language

Language has been identified as an important issue. Job-stereotyping can be avoided – feminists point out that it is easy to substitute 'police officer' for 'policeman' – although we acknowledge some of the difficulties that can arise when this process produces ugly and false-sounding words. Other teachers have discussed their strategies to avoid using the generic 'he' or 'man', since this can have the effect of making women disappear (Spender, 1979). Skilful alterations to the words of songs are made; for instance, when 'Miss Polly had a dolly who was sick, sick, sick/And she called for the doctor to come quick, quick, quick', it was a female and not a male doctor who responded.

Creating a 'fair deal' for girls in the classroom

Teachers have experimented with a range of teaching strategies to give girls a 'fair deal' in the classroom and to reduce the amount of teacher attention that boys get. These include avoiding 'up front' class teaching, which militates against girls because boys demand and get more teacher time. Small-group work makes an equitable division of attention easier. Teachers have cut whole-class discussions to a minimum; if the class is broken into small groups for talk and learning it facilitates girls and quieter boys talking and learning. Teachers have monitored the time they spend with pupils in the classroom and insisted on a fair distribution of time.

Teachers in secondary education have experimented with strategies designed to encourage girls to feel more free to participate in classroom discussions. Some schools have carried out investigations into who does most of the talking in a classroom. It is relatively easy to keep a record over a week or so, and it was discovered that, when they realize the imbalance, girls will frequently begin to tackle the boys about it.

Another approach is to give girls extra space and time to develop public speaking confidence and skills. In one school, a room between two classes became the 'girls' room'. Meetings were held there on a weekly basis to discuss equal opportunities. The girls expressed their approval of the scheme, finding that it gave them greater confidence to participate in whole-class discussions.

Some teachers have campaigned against sexual harassment in their schools, with varying degrees of success (Ord and Quigley, 1985). They have raised the issue at staff meetings and aimed to persuade the school to take the issue seriously and to adopt anti-sexist guidelines. One school kept an incident book in which assaults and abuse were recorded; the headteacher then used assemblies to make public announcements about reprimands to boys whose names appeared in the book (Jones, 1985). One London school established morning tutorials for single-sex discussions. The graffiti in the school provided a good starting point for these.

One important strategy has been that of developing support groups both for women teachers and also for pupils. The DASI project in London, for example, worked to help girls develop both awareness of the problems and the confidence to tackle them together. The aim was to encourage girls to offer each other support against any harassment that occurred in the school (Cornbleet and Libovitch, 1983). Feminist teachers stress the importance of ensuring that individual groups are involved in a network. Organizations like the Women in Education Group and CASSOE (Campaign Against Sexism and Sexual Oppression in Education) provide support and ideas for teachers, and their newsletters, *GEN* and *CASSOE*, can help prevent school groups from feeling isolated (see Appendix 1 for details).

The hidden curriculum: an assessment of the strategies

Strategies to improve on the discriminatory practices that occur in the hidden curriculum are difficult to evaluate, as so much comes down to the way individual teachers handle their classes. It is very much a question of attitudes; as one teacher put it:

> Being a feminist teacher in a classroom is not just a matter of introducing positive images of women wherever possible or of devoting a three week period in a year to a discussion of sexism in society, it is a matter of constantly questioning the way teacher and students make sense of a patriarchal world. (Payne, 1980, p. 174)

There are clearly many committed teachers aiming to work in new and fair ways with children in their charge. In some LEAs there are clear and well-established guidelines and policies which encourage good processes and practice, and are committed to removing discrimination. However, this is not true of all areas of Britain, and there remains significant apathy and resistance to the issue.

External examinations and assessment

There has been substantial change in the external examinations system with the introduction of GCSE. Evidence is beginning to emerge that girls' performance in the new system is improving in relation to boys'. The GCSE results for the last three years have recently been broken down according to gender (Table 8.2), and the figures analysed show a number of interesting developments (Stobart, Elwood and Quinlon, forthcoming).

Table 8.2 Total numbers of candidates entering GCSE examinations, and percentage of GCSE passes (grades A–C) in given subjects achieved by candidates, 1990*

	Percentage gaining grades A–C		Total number	
	Girls	Boys	Girls	Boys
Maths	43.0	42.9	341 170	322 513
Physics	56.3	52.3	55 247	134 749
Combined science	48.1	50.8	84 607	95 273
CDT	42.4	38.4	4 119	36 710
History	52.3	46.3	117 371	112 131
Home economics	41.0	22.5	131 939	18 504

* Note that the girls' and boys' results added together do not total 100 per cent, because we have given figures only for those who achieved grades A to C.
Source: GCSE Inter-Group Statistics for summer 1990.

In English and foreign languages girls continue to outperform boys, and we have not included these figures. In mathematics, boys still do better than girls, because they still obtain more of the higher grades (A and B) than girls. There is evidence that schools only enter girls for the intermediate level of maths GCSE, which means they cannot achieve above a grade C. However, girls are improving their results in mathematics overall, in terms of the number of passes gained.

In physics, girls are gaining a higher percentage of A–C grades than boys, but we have to note that the overall number of girls who are entered for physics is tiny in comparison to the number of boys. It is still a predominantly male subject and the girls who take it are heavily selected by schools. However, this is not the case for combined science GCSE, where the numbers of boys and girls are comparable.

Stobart, Elwood and Quinlon conclude that girls' improved performance in GCSE is directly related to the weight allocated to and the type of coursework set by the subject. The more coursework a subject requires the better girls do. In this context it is interesting to note that most GCSE maths syllabuses are reluctant to incorporate much coursework (Stobart, Elwood and Quinlon, forthcoming). If they were to do so it is likely that there could be improvements in girls' performance in maths. (At the time of writing the prime minister has announced a move back to traditional end-of-course examinations, at which boys do better than girls.)

While there are some signs of improvement, we are not suggesting that the problem is solved. The old GCE/CSE external examination system was accused of sex bias. The Fawcett Society concluded that some examination boards had made more effort to correct the bias, and some subject areas showed more awareness of the problem, than others. The London Examination Board declared its determination to improve the situation, but other English boards seemed largely unaware of equal opportunity issues. We do not as yet have the research to show whether the examination boards involved in GCSE have improved on sex bias in their syllabuses or in the questions asked in examination papers. There is clearly work to be done in influencing external examining bodies to place equal opportunities on their agenda, especially as GCSE develops.

Classroom assessment

Not all assessment goes on in external examinations, and with the development of new classroom testing procedures in the National Curriculum the equal opportunities implications need to be carefully monitored. There are a number of new developments in assessment, and feminist researchers and teachers have expressed some concern about the differential effect these can have on boys and girls. In the ILEA Records of Achievement scheme a number of issues were identified in relation to 'profiling'. Profiling requires pupils to be clear about their own achievements and strengths, and pupils have to emphasize their strengths to their teaching staff. Research suggests that this may be more difficult for girls to do than for boys.

Conclusion

The area of assessment and equal opportunities is a new one and it is important that the findings of recent research are disseminated through the education system. Teachers can adopt less biased strategies in their internal assessment, but it is also the case that pressure needs to be put upon the external examining authorities to promote change.

The world of work and careers advice

Classroom strategies

Feminist secondary school teachers have introduced equal opportunity concerns into their teaching on the 'world of work'. They have encouraged pupils to ask questions about employment prospects for girls and boys, and identified the restrictions that operate for both sexes. Wages are another fruitful area for class discussion; for example, on why women earn less than men despite the effects of equal pay legislation.

The careers service

Government has given the careers service a strong indication of the importance of equal opportunities, and a number of publications and guidelines have been provided. Coles and Maynard (1990) looked at how effective they are. They concluded that the implementation was patchy, and greater resources for training and projects are necessary.

Employers

Others have made the point that employers too can have a role. Some employers have been willing to host and organize talks on the fact that boys and girls are equally needed in their company (Nestlé in Croydon; EOC/London Borough of Croydon 1985, p. 54).

Programmes to implement change: conclusions

In this section we have looked at the range of programmes that have been tried out by national bodies, by local authorities and by individual schools and teachers. We need to be cautious in assessing how much effect all of this activity has had. There have been successes; equal opportunities are firmly on the agenda in many schools and LEAs. However, these achievements do not indicate a groundswell of sustained or active concern among teachers or education policy-makers.

PROBLEMS WITH WHAT HAS ALREADY BEEN DONE

Equal opportunity work has achieved some success, but it is possible to identify a number of problems with what has already been done in Britain. The main criticisms are that the government has not been sufficiently committed to equal opportunities, which means that it is not taken seriously enough in many local authorities and schools. There are also theoretical problems with some of the equal opportunities initiatives.

A national initiative

A great deal of the work done on equal opportunities (gender) in Britain has been dependent on what Lynda Carr, the principal education officer of the EOC, called 'principle and personal commitment' (Carr, 1989, p. 164). The fact that equal opportunities initiatives got off the ground at all is the result of the individual commitment of teachers implementing ad hoc practical strategies.

There are problems with this approach. First, such ad hoc programmes are difficult to monitor and evaluate systematically. (For an account of one exception – Leicestershire LEA's evaluation – see Skelton, 1989.) In addition, individual teachers who are committed to change can rapidly feel overwhelmed by the odds against being able to do anything meaningful in this field. The central problem has been that these committed teachers are not by and large in senior positions where they can have a significant influence on the policies of the whole school. Small-scale changes can have significant effects, but it is possible to suggest that we need more nationally agreed and co-ordinated plans and actions with a properly resourced base.

In other western countries governments have been prepared to intervene in education to promote social equality. In Sweden and some Canadian states, the government has backed national equal opportunity initiatives. The United Kingdom has taken a much more cautious line, as has Spain (Weiner, 1990). Weiner informs us that there is now an EEC working group on gender equality in education. They will make recommendations on programmes which will apply across Europe, and it is possible that the British government may be provoked into taking more action as a result (Weiner, 1990).

There has been criticism of what the British government has done to improve gender equality in education. The initiatives have all taken a liberal approach and followed the equal opportunities model. As a result radical and socialist feminist groups have been disparaging about the schemes, claiming that they cannot achieve any significant change. In addition, there is a suggestion that in the current situation the focus of equal opportunities work may narrow significantly. The main aim will become one of widening employment opportunities for girls and women, specifically of getting a greater proportion of girls into technology. This is part of a more general policy of regenerating the economy and of wealth creation. This significantly reduces the aim of bringing about greater gender equality in education.

There are criticisms to be made of the equal opportunities work which has been implemented in the UK, but it has had successes too.

Current research and evaluation of what has been done both indicate some fruitful strategies for the future.

WAYS FORWARD IN THE FUTURE

Recent research has been interested in a number of areas. Detailed analysis has been made of the ages at which children are most receptive to equal opportunities work, and there is interest in finding better ways to educate boys. Effective equal opportunities work requires planning and resourcing, and an essential aspect is including teachers in the change. Feminist groups have also reopened the debate about co-education and have asserted the value of single-sex schooling.

Focused interventions

Current research work is beginning to make it clear that gender socialization and the development of sex role stereotypes occur in stages for children. On the basis of this information we are in a better position to know what the best ages are for introducing intervention work with pupils. Short and Carrington concluded that the developmental progression implies that

> DIRECT teaching about occupational stereotypes may be optimally effective if it commences for the generality of children about the age of eight. The age of ten to eleven is when the majority of children are most receptive to explicit teaching about the role of the family in replicating this form of inequality. (Short and Carrington, 1989, p. 37)

Research findings of this kind can make an impact on practice, creating a more focused approach.

Finding better ways to educate boys

So far much of the equal opportunities work has intended to remedy the discrimination that girls encounter in schools. It is clear that boys too face disadvantages. One of the newest areas of emphasis is on finding appropriate anti-sexist strategies for educating boys as well as girls. In order to do this feminists consider that questions about how we define masculinity and about the self-image of boys and their sexual identity need to be asked. Arnot demands that we look for ways of reducing sexism in school by developing new and positive forms of masculinity that do not depend on the devaluing of women (Arnot, 1984). Reay (1990) gives a detailed description of useful classroom strategies that she has tried out.

143

Integrating equal opportunities

The successful implementation of an equal opportunities policy rests on engaging the co-operation of teachers. Policies imposed from outside tend to be regarded as a threat to teacher's professionalism, whatever the area of change. A necessary condition for success is the pursuit of an integrated rather than an add-on approach: equal opportunities cannot just be bolted on. Teachers have to be persuaded from the beginning that equal opportunities can and should be delivered as a part of normal curriculum activity. The research we have reveals very clearly the extent and depth of the antagonism and apathy that exist in our schools about this issue. It is apparent that whatever strategies and models are chosen, it is important to move slowly and not to antagonize staff or parents at the school.

Co-education

Some feminist groups assert that the only effective way forward is to return to a system of single-sex schools, at least for the 11–16 age group. The debate about co-education has a long history, but seemed settled by policy changes in the 1960s and 1970s. Since comprehensive reorganization, over three-quarters of all children are educated in mixed sex schools. In recent years, feminists have supported single-sex education in the light of current demands for equal educational opportunities.

There is evidence that girls' academic achievement is better overall in single-sex schools (Dale, 1969, 1971, 1974). There is also evidence that girls are more willing to take science subjects when they are in single-sex schools (DES, 1975, p. 12). However, most of the information we have was collected from selective schools, where we would expect academic results to be better.

The other arguments about single-sex schooling centre around the social advantages that derive from educating the sexes together, and there is no agreement on this. Liberal thinking is that educating boys and girls prepares them for life together and facilitates good relationships in adult life. Many feminists argue that in schools girls learn that boys have more power than they do, and they learn subordination. Single-sex schools provide a freer environment for girls to learn alternative and stronger roles.

CONCLUSION

Equal opportunities are now on the agenda of some schools and some colleges, but a great deal remains to be done. Failure to take on board gender issues is a very serious omission. The number of young people qualified to enter those expanding areas of the economy where there are skill shortages will not increase, and the fulfilment of individual potential which has always been at the heart of a good educational system will continue to be lost to the majority of the nation.

> The needs of the nation and the needs of the individual are wisely reconciled by a good equal opportunities policy where concepts of economic value and social justice have equal weight. (Carr, 1989, p. 19)

CHAPTER SUMMARY

In this chapter we have looked at the range of national, local and school-based initiatives for change in the area of equal opportunities (gender). A number of strategies have been tried out on an ad hoc and experimental basis. There is little systematic evaluation of what has been done, and it is difficult to assess how much progress has been made.

SUGGESTIONS FOR FURTHER READING

Equal opportunities (gender) issues

Arnot, M. and Weiner, G. (eds) (1989) *Gender and the Politics of Schooling*. London: Hutchinson.

Burchell, H. and Millman. V. (eds) (1987) *Changing Perspectives on Gender*. Milton Keynes: Open University Press. A full account of many of the new initiatives that have been launched at secondary level, such as TVEI, TRIST and LAPP.

Curriculum innovations

Burchell, H. and Millman, V. (eds) (1989) *Changing Perspectives on Gender*. Milton Keynes: Open University Press. See under 'Equal opportunities (gender) issues' above.

Delamont, S. (1990) *Sex Roles and the School*. London: Routledge. The last chapter of the book has a detailed and accessible account of the Women's Training Roadshows.

Equal Opportunities Commission (EOC) (1988) *Gender Issues: The Implications for Schools of the Education Reform Act 1988*. Manchester: EOC.

ILEA (1982) Sex Differences and Achievement. *Research and Statistical Report RS 823/82*. London: ILEA.

Kant, L. (1989) National Curriculum: notionally equal. *NUT Education Review*, **1** (2).

NFER (1989) *Equal Opportunities for Girls and Boys within TVEI*. Sheffield: Training Agency. This is the 'official' evaluation of the entire TVEI scheme. It contains a comprehensive account of many different intervention strategies that have been tried out across the equal opportunities (gender) field.

NUT (1989) Equal opportunities in the new ERA. *NUT Education Review*, **3** (2).

Peacock, S. and Shinkins, S. (1983) *Insight: A Review of the Insight Programme to Encourage More Girls to Become Professional Engineers*. Engineering Industry Training Board.

Sims, D. (1987) Work experience in TVEI: student views and reactions. In S.M. Hinkley, (1987) *The TVEI Experience*. Sheffield: MSC.

Skelton, C. (ed.) (1989) *Whatever Happens to Little Women?* Milton Keynes: Open University Press. A useful account of a range of classroom interventions at primary school level.

Tutchell, E. (ed.) (1990) *Dolls and Dungarees*. Milton Keynes: Open University Press. A set of practitioner accounts of classroom-based intervention strategies.

Curriculum and boys

EOC (1982) *Report of Conference on Equal Opportunities: What's in It for Boys*. Manchester: EOC.

Assessment

Burchell, H. and Millman, V. (eds) (1987) *Changing Perspectives on Gender*. Milton Keynes: Open University Press. See under 'Equal opportunities (gender) issues' above.

Lines, A. (1989) *Guidance and Profiling within TVEI*. Windsor: NFER for the Training Agency.

Careers advice

Equal Opportunities Commission (EOC) (1983) *A Guide to the Equal Treatment of the Sexes in Careers Material*. Manchester: EOC.

Co-education

Deem, R. (ed.) (1984) *Co-education Reconsidered*. Milton Keynes: Open University Press.

Sarah, E., Scott, M. and Spender, D. (1980) The education of feminists: the case for single-sex schools. In D. Spender and E. Sarah (eds), *Learning to Lose*. London: Women's Press.

APPENDIX 1

Resources

CURRICULUM MATERIALS

English literature

Children's Rights Workshop (1987) *Sexism in Children's Books: Facts, Figures and Guidelines*. London: Writers' and Readers' Publishing Co-operative.

Leeson, R. (1985) *Reading and Righting: The Past, Present and Future of Fiction for the Young*. London: Collins.

Miller, C. and Swift, K. (1981) *The Handbook of Non-sexist Writing*. Women's Press.

Stones, R. (1983) *Pour out the Cocoa Janet: Sexism in Children's Books*. London: Longman.

Stones, R. (1985) *Ms. Muffet Fights Back: A Penguin Non-sexist Booklist*. Harmondsworth: Penguin.

Language

National Association for the Teaching of English, 8 Burley School Annex, Fox Lane Site, Frechville, Sheffield S12 4WY. NATE produces a number of publications, for example:

NATE (1985) *Alice in Genderland: Reflections on Language, Power and Control*. Sheffield: NATE.

Miller, C. and Swift, K. (1981) *Handbook of Non-sexist Writing for Writers, Editors and Speakers*. London: Women's Press.

Foreign language teaching

Assessment and Performance Unit (1986) *Foreign Language Performance in Schools*. London: APU.

Beswick, C. (1976) Mixed or single sex for French. *Audio Visual Language Journal*, **15** (1), 34–8.

Dunbar, C. (1987) Languages. In K. Myers (ed.), *Genderwatch*. London: EOC/SCDC.

History

Hufton, O. (1988) What is Women's History? In J. Gardiner (ed), *What Is History Today?* London: Macmillan. This brief and clear statement about the field of feminist history is a useful introduction for teachers.

Warnock, K. (1988) *Mary Wollstonecraft*. London: Hamish Hamilton. In the 'In Her Own Time' series of history books for secondary school pupils. An interesting idea in some ways, but it is possible to criticize it for simply replacing the 'great men' approach to history with 'great women'.

Dictionary of Women's Biography (1984) London: Macmillan.

Adams, C. (1983) Off the record. *Teaching History*, **36** (June).

Adams, C. (1984) Equal opportunities: gender. *Clio*, **4** (3) (available from History and Social Sciences Teachers Centre, 377 Clapham Road, London SW9).

(1984) Her Studies: A Resource List for Teachers of History and Social Sciences (available from History and Social Sciences Teachers Centre, 377 Clapham Road, London SW9).

ILEA (1990) *Social Studies in the Primary School* (available from Harcourt, Brace Jovanovich Ltd, ILEA Learning Resources Branch, FREEPOST, Foots Cray High Street, Sidcup, Kent DA14 4BR).

ILEA (1990) *History in the Primary School*. London: Harcourt, Brace Jovanovich.

(1986) History and Social Sciences: Teacher's Centre review. *Clio*, **6** (1).

Geography

Bale, J.R. (1982) Sexism in geographic education. In A. Kent (ed.), *Bias in Geographic Education*. London: Institute of Education.

Connolly, J. (1987) Geography. In K. Myers (ed.), *Genderwatch*. London: EOC/SCDC.

Hughes, P. (1987) Time to get girl friendly: geography. *TES*, 4 December 1987.

Larsen, B. (1983) The gender gap in the geography curriculum. In *Geography and Education for a Multicultural Society* (conference report). London: University of London Institute of Education.

Slater, F. (1983) Sexism and racism: parallel experiences: an exploration. *Geography and Education for a Multicultural Society* (conference report). London: University of London Institute of Education.

Mathematics

Open University/ILEA (1986) *Girls into Mathematics*. Cambridge: Cambridge University Press. This is a study pack aimed at secondary schools, but primary teachers would also find it valuable. It could be used by an individual or more usefully by a group.

Walden, R. and Walkerdine, V. (1982) *Girls and Mathematics: The Early Years*. Bedford Way Papers 8. University of London, Institute of Education.

Walden, R. and Walkerdine, V. (1985) *Girls and Mathematics: From Primary to Secondary Schooling*. Bedford Way Papers 24. University of London, Institute of Education.

These two booklets were written as the result of detailed observations in schools. They are theoretical and not always easy to read, but are worth looking at for analysis of fundamental issues.

Eddowes, M. (1983) *Humble Pi: The Mathematical Education of Girls*. London: Longman, for the Schools Council. This again provides a useful review of research in both primary and secondary schools.

Burton, L. (ed.) (1986) *Girls into Maths Can Go*. Eastbourne: Holt, Rinehart and Winston. This collection of articles forms the reader for the Open University *Girls into Maths* pack, but is well worth looking at for its own sake. There is a secondary bias, but most of the articles have general interest and some refer explicitly to primary school.

Drake, P. (1987) Mathematics. In K. Myers (ed.), *Genderwatch*. London: EOC/SCDC.

GAMMA (Gender and Mathematics Association) is a national association in the UK, which has produced a newsletter since it was founded in 1981. A national conference has been held each year in different parts of the country, and local GAMMA groups put on occasional day and half-day conferences in their own areas. For more information contact: GAMMA, c/o Department of Mathematical Sciences, Goldsmiths' College, New Cross, London SE14 6NW. They have also produced a bibliography:

Girls and Mathematics Association (undated) *Girls and Mathematics Association Bibliography* (available free of charge from GAMMA).

IOWME (International Organization of Women and Mathematics Education) was formed in 1976, and held international conferences of mathematical education. Since 1985 it has produced a bi-annual news letter. GAMMA (see above) is also the contact point for IOWME.

Centre for Science and Maths Education, Chelsea College, University of London, Bridges Place, London SW6 4HR.

Science

Smail, B. (1984) *Girl Friendly Science: Avoiding Sex Bias in the Curriculum*. London: Longman.

The Association for Science Education, College Lane, Hatfield, Herts AL10 9AA.

ASE deals with the issue of gender and science teaching in its journal from time to time. It has also produced sets of teaching materials which are 'girl-friendly'.

Centre for the Study of Comprehensive Schools, Wentworth College, University of York, York YO1 5DD.

The centre has a databank of entries of interesting practice on equal opportunities in schools.

CFL VISION, PO Box 35, Wetherby, Yorks LS23 7EX.

This company distributes films on behalf of the EOC. Their films include one on women in physics and one entitled *What Are You Really Made Of?* which encourages school leavers to try non-traditional occupations. Another, *Technology Starts Here*, is about introducing technology to 9–13-year-olds.

Department of Trade and Industry, Equality in Education Division, Room 340, Kingsgate House, 66–74 Victoria Street, London SW1E 6SW.

The DTI has a (free) catalogue of videos which can be used in schools, including videos on girls and engineering.

Equal Opportunities Commission, Overseas House, Quay Street, Manchester M3 3HN.

The EOC has a catalogue of publications, posters, videos and films about girls and sciences, technology, information technology and mathematics.

The Engineering Industry Training Board, Engineering Careers Information Service, 54 Clarendon Road, Watford, Herts WD1 1LB.

The EITB has a special WISE edition of 'Careers in British Engineering'.

Computing and information technology

Equal Opportunities Commission (EOC) (1985) *Girls and Information Technology: A Report of a Project in the London Borough of Croydon to Evaluate Good Practice in the IT Curriculum*. Manchester: EOC.

EOC (1985) *Info Tech and Gender: An Overview*. Manchester: EOC.

Jennings, M. and Smits, J. (1986) *Women's Computing Course: A Teaching Pack* (available from 157 Maryland Road, London, N22 5AS.

Art, music, drama

Bachman, D.G. and Piland, S. (eds) (1979) *Women Artists: A Historical, Contemporary and Feminist Bibliography*. Metuchen, NJ: Scarecrow Press.

Connolly, J. and Garb, T. (1987) Art. In K. Myers (ed.), *Genderwatch*. London: EOC/SCDC.

Dodgson, E. (1987) Drama. In K. Myers (ed.), *Genderwatch*. London: EOC/SCDC.

Dodgson, E. (1982) Exploring social issues. In J. Nixon (ed.), *Drama and the Whole Curriculum*. London: Hutchinson.

Griffiths, V. (1984) Feminist research and the use of drama. *Women's Studies International Journal*, 7 (6).

Griffiths, V. (1986) *Using Drama to Get at Gender*. Manchester: University of Manchester.

Jobbins, V. (1987) Dance. In K. Myers (ed.), *Genderwatch*. London: EOC/SCDC.

Joyce, K. (1982) *Sex Stereotyping Explored through Drama*. Manchester: Manchester Teachers' Centre.

McNiff, K. (1982) Sex differences in children's art. *Journal of Education*, **164** (3).

Wills, G. (1987) Music. In K. Myers (ed.), *Genderwatch*. London: EOC/SCDC.

Sport and physical education

Browne, P., Metzen, L. and Whyld, J. (1983) Physical education. In J. Whyld (ed.), *Sexism in the Secondary Curriculum*. London: Harper and Row.

Carrington, B. (1986) Equal opportunities and physical education. In J. Evans (ed.), *Physical Education, Sport and Schooling*. Lewes: Falmer Press.

Coventry Curriculum Development (1982) *Physical Education in a Multicultural Society*. Coventry: Elm Bank Teachers' Centre.

Coventry Curriculum Development (1982) *Cultural Diversity: A Role for Physical Education*. Coventry: Elm Bank Teachers' Centre.

Graydon, J. (1987) Physical Education. In K. Myers (ed.), *Genderwatch*. London: EOC/SCDC.

Graydon, J., Gilroy, S. and Webb, S. (1985) Mixed Physical Education in the Secondary School; An Evaluation. Paper presented to ICHPER, World Congress, WLIHE in July.

Hall, M.A. (1987) *Women's Studies International Forum Special Issue: The Gendering of Sport, Leisure and Physical Education*. Oxford: Pergamon Press.

Issue on Gender (1986) *British Journal of Physical Education*, **17** (4).

PE: Who cares? *Sports Woman Magazine* (published monthly: available from Womensports Ltd, BCM Womensports, London WC1N 3XX).

Scraton, S. (1984) Mixed Physical Education Teaching in Secondary Education: A Progressive Move for Girls. Paper presented to Girl-Friendly Schooling Conference, Manchester.

Religious education

Hanlon, D. (1987) Religious education. In K. Myers (ed.), *Genderwatch*. London: EOC/SCDC.

King, U. (1987) World religions, women and education. *Comparative Education*, **23** (1), 35–49.

ILEA (1990) *Religious Education for Our Children* (available from Harcourt, Brace Jovanovich Ltd, ILEA Learning Resources Branch, FREEPOST, Foots Cray High Street, Sidcup, Kent DA14 4BR).

Sex education

Cousins, J. (1980) *Make It Happy: What Sex Is All About*. Harmondsworth: Penguin.

See Red Women's Workshop, 90A Camberwell Road, Camberwell, London SE5 produces posters with positive images of women in the field of sex education.

Adams, C., Fay, J. and Loreen-Martin, J. (1987) *No Is Not Enough, Helping Teenagers Avoid Sexual Assault*. Impact Books, California.

The Health Education Council and the National Children's Bureau keep longer lists of helpful materials.

Massey, D. (1987) Health education. In K. Myers (ed.), *Genderwatch*. London: EOC/SCDC.

National Council for One-parent Families (no date) *Pregnant at School* (available from 255 Kentish Town Road, London NW5 2LX).

Shapiro, C.H. (1980) Sexual learning: the short-changed adolescent male. *Social Work*, **25** (6).

Slavin, H. (1986) *Greater Expectations: A Source Book for Working with Women and Girls*. London: Learning Development Aids.

Special education

'A concern about sex equitable education for disabled students' (1983) Concerns, 1X (available from CCSSO Resource Centre Sex Equity Suite, 379, 400N Capital Street NW, Washington DC 20001, USA).

Campling, J. (ed.) (1981) *Images of Ourselves: Women with Disabilities Talking*. London: Routledge & Kegan Paul.

Deegan, M.J. and Brooks, N.A. (1985) *Women and Disability: The Double Handicap*. Transaction Books.

Warner, S. and K. Myers, (1987) Special educational needs. In K. Myers (ed.), *Genderwatch*. London: EOC/SCDC.

Winter, M. (1983) Remedial education. In J. Whyld (ed.), *Sexism in the Secondary Curriculum*. London: Harper & Row.

Domestic science and child development

David, M. (1987) The dilemmas of parent education and parental skills for sexual equality. In S. Walker and L. Barton (eds), *Changing Policies, Changing Teachers*: Milton Keynes: Open University Press.

Thompson, P.J. (1984) Beyond gender: equity issues for home economics education. *Theory into Practice* (Autumn), 276–83.

Wadsworth, N. (1987) Home economics and child development. In K. Myers (ed.), *Genderwatch*. London: EOC/SCDC.

Wynn, B. (1977) Domestic subjects and the sexual division of labour. In *E202, Schooling and Society: Units 14–15*. Milton Keynes: Open University Press.

Wynn, B. (1983) Home economics. In J. Whyld (ed.), *Sexism in the Secondary Curriculum*. London: Harper and Row.

ILEA (1990) *Food: A Resource for Learning in the Primary School* (available from Harcourt, Brace Jovanovich Ltd, ILEA Learning Resources Branch, FREEPOST, Foots Cray High Street, Sidcup, Kent DA14 4BR).

Assemblies

Beddoe, D. (1983) *Discovering Women's History: A Practical Handbook*. London: Pandora.

Hoy, L. and M. (1985) *An Alternative Assembly Book*. London: Longman.

Profitt, R. (1983) *Assembly Book: Assemblies for Our Multi-racial Society*. London: Longman.

Teaching equal opportunities issues

Carrington, B. and Troyna, B. (1988) *Children and Controversial Issues: Strategies for the Early and Middle Years*. Lewes: Falmer Press.

Coussins, J. (no date) *Taking Liberties: A Teaching Pack for Girls and Boys on Equal Rights*. London: National Council for Civil Liberties.

Berheide, C.W. and Segal, M.T. (1985) Teaching sex and gender: a decade of experience. *Teaching Sociology*, 12 (3), 267–83.

Kirton, A. (1983) Teaching a women's rights course in a secondary school. *Feminist Review*, 15, 81–9.

Mahony, P. (1983) Boys will be boys: teaching women's studies in a mixed-sex group. *Women's Studies International Forum*, 6 (3), 331–4.

Yates, L. (1986) Is Women's Studies a legitimate school subject? An outline of an agenda for discussion. *Journal of Curriculum Studies*, **18** (1).

Careers education

Agnew, D. (1987) Careers. In K. Myers (ed.), *Genderwatch*. London: EOC/SCDC.

Avent, C. (1982) Careers education and guidance. *Secondary Education Journal*, **12** (2), 6–7.

Benett, Y. Training opportunities: how fair are they for young women? *Training Officer*, **18** (7), 182–3.

Chisholm, L.A. and Holland, J. (1986) Girls and occupational choice: anti-sexism in action in a curriculum development project. *British Journal of Sociology of Education*, **7** (4), 353–66.

The Young Women's Christian Association (1987) *Girls in Male Jobs: A Research Report* (available from YWCA Headquarters, Clarendon House, 52 Cornmarket Street, Oxford OX1 3EJ).

Trades Union Congress (1987) *The Education and Training of Girls and Women* (available from TUC Publications Dept, Congress House, 42 Russell Street, London WCIB 3LS).

Watts, T. and Kant, L. (1986) *A Working Start: Guidance Strategies for Girls and Young Women*. Harlow : Longman.

National Advisory Centre on Careers for Women, Drayton House, 30 Gordon Street, London WC1H OAX.

EQUAL OPPORTUNITIES POLICIES

The EOC has produced booklets which provide guidelines on the Sex Discrimination legislation, and providing equal opportunities in schools:

An Equal Start deals with the under-fives.

Do You Provide Equal Educational Opportunities? looks at secondary and further education.

Equal Opportunities in Post-School Education deals with higher and further education.

The Advisory Centre for Education also has a number of information sheets which are useful:

(1984) 'Sex Discrimination and the School Governor'.

(1984) 'Sex Discrimination in Education'.

Foster, M., Smith, S. and Brooking, C. (1987) *Teaching for Equality: Educational Resources on Race and Gender*. London: Runnymede Trust.

Klein, S.S. (1985) *Handbook for Achieving Sex Equity through Education*. Baltimore: Johns Hopkins Press.

ILEA produced a number of accounts of their equal opportunities policies and schemes, now available from Harcourt, Brace Jovanovich Ltd, ILEA Learning Resources branch, FREEPOST, Foots Cray High Street, Sidcup, Kent DA14 4BR:

Race, Sex and Class (1990). This is a pack of six booklets which provides help to all schools wishing to formulate their own anti-racist and anti-sexist policies. Many deal with both gender, and race, and there is one entitled 'A Policy for Equality: Sex'.

Implementing the ILEA's Anti-sexist Policy: A Guide for Schools (1990). This is a companion volume to *Race, Sex and Class*.

Primary Matters: Some Approaches to Equal Opportunities in Primary Schools (1990). This book is a collection of eighty first-hand accounts of equal opportunities strategies and initiatives that teachers tried out in nursery and primary schools.

SEXUAL HARASSMENT

Jones, C. (1985) Sexual tyranny: male violence in a mixed secondary school. In G. Weiner (ed.), *Just a Bunch of Girls*. Milton Keynes: Open University Press.

Lees, S. (1983) How boys slag off girls. *New Society*, **13**.

Lees, S. (1986) *Losing Out: Sexuality and the Adolescent Girl*. London: Hutchinson.

Cassoe (Campaign Against Sexism and Sexual Oppression in Education), 17 Lymington Road, London, NW6. Newsletter six times a year.

Women in Education Group, c/o M. Anderson, 99 Psalter Avenue, Sheffield S11 8YP.

Women and Education Newsletter Collective, 14 St Brendan's Road, Withington, Manchester 20.

MASCULINITIES

Cockburn, C. (1983) *Brothers, Male Dominance and Technological Change*. London: Pluto Press.

Connell, R.W. (1983) *Which Way Is Up? Essays on Class, Sex and Culture*. London: Allen and Unwin.

Metcalf, A. and Humphries, M. (1985) (eds) *The Sexuality of Men*. London: Pluto Press.

FINDING BETTER WAYS TO EDUCATE BOYS

ILEA (1984) *Equal Opportunities: What's In It for Boys? Materials for Teachers*. Hackney Teachers' Centre: ILEA.

Askew, S. and Ross, C. (1988) *Boys Don't Cry: Boys and Sexism in Education*. Milton Keynes: Open University Press.

TEACHERS AND GENDER ISSUES

Burgess, R.G. (1988) Points and posts: teacher careers in a comprehensive school. In A. Green and S. Ball (eds), *Progress and Inequality in Comprehensive Education*. London: Routledge. This gives an ethnographic account of teachers' appointments to a physical education post.

Burgess, R.G. (1989) Something you learn to live with? Gender and inequality in a comprehensive school. *Gender and Education*, 1 (2).

Burgess, H. (1989) A sort of career: women in primary schools. In C. Skelton, (ed.), *Whatever Happens to Little Women?* Milton Keynes: Open University Press.

Lawn, M. and Grace, G. (eds) (1987) *Teachers: The Culture and Politics of Work*. Lewes: Falmer. This book provides an account of teachers as an occupational group. There are papers on the historical context, on contemporary work, on the politics of work and on teachers and the state. See especially the essays by Joyce and by Steedman.

Adams, C. (1985) Teachers' attitudes towards issues of sex equality. In J. Whyte *et al.* (eds), *Girl-Friendly Schooling*. London: Methuen.

Bloomfield, J. and O'Hara, R. (1983) *Equal Opportunities Teaching and Teacher-training Courses* (available from Centre for Institutional Studies, NELPCO, Danbury Park, Chelmsford, Essex).

EOC (1982) *Women and Teaching: The Way Ahead*. Manchester: EOC.

Women's Advisory Committee, TUC, Congress House, Great Russell House, London WC1B 3LS.

Race and gender

Arnot, M. (1985) *Equal Opportunities Policies in Education*. Oxford: Pergamon Press.

Open University (1985) Race and Gender and Education Policy Making. *Course E333, Module 4*. Milton Keynes: Open University Press.

ORGANIZATIONS

Equal Opportunities Commission, Overseas House, Quay Street, Manchester M3 3HN.

The EOC has published a great deal of material that can be useful for teachers about the different kinds of problem that exist in British schools.

Fawcett Library, City of London Polytechnic, Old Castle Street, London E1 7NT.

Letterbox Library, 1st floor, 5 Bradbury Street, London N16 8JN. Children's book club specializing in non-sexist books.

Feminist Library, Hungerford House, Victoria Embankment, London WC2 6PA.

JOURNALS

Gender and Education, Carfax Publishing Company, PO Box 25, Abingdon, Oxfordshire OX14 3UE. 1989 onwards, three issues a year. Specialist journal on feminist educational issues.

Equality Now, EOC Publications Section, Overseas House, Quay Street, Manchester M3 3HN. 1983 onwards, quarterly; see also the EOC catalogue of publications and their *The Fact about Women Is* (free annually).

Feminist Review, 11 Carleton Gardens, Brecknock Road, London, N19 5AQ. 1979 onwards, three issues per annum.

Feminist Studies, Women's Studies Program, University of Maryland, College Park, MD 20742. 1972 onwards, three issues per annum.

Women's Studies International Forum, Pergamon Press. 1978 onwards, bi-monthly.

Women's Studies Newsletter, Women's Education Advisory Committee, Workers Education Association. Two issues per annum.

AUDIOVISUAL AIDS

Cinema of Women, Unit 160, 27 Clerkenwell Close, London EC1R OAT.

EOC (Visual Aids), Central Film Library, Chalfont Grove, Gerrards Cross, Buckinghamshire SL9 8TN.

BIBLIOGRAPHIES

Weiner, G. and Arnot, M. (eds) (1988) *Gender and Education Bibliography*. Milton Keynes: Open University Press.

Britton, M.C. (1991) *Improved Visibility: An International Bibliography for the Education of Women and Girls 1978–1989*. Librarians of Institutes and Schools of Education (available from Brotherton Library, University of Leeds, Leeds, L52 1JT).

Equal opportunities policies

Equal opportunities policies vary a great deal. Some are precise and designed to cover all areas of school life, as far as possible. Others are much more general and have little to say about the types of action that will be taken to attempt to ensure equal opportunities. It may be that the degree of specificity of a policy indicates the degree of commitment to equal opportunities within a school.

In this book we have examples of both precise and general policies. Edgewick Community Primary School in Coventry is happy for us to use its name and we are grateful to the staff and governors for allowing us to present their policy. The other policy comes from Billsdyck Secondary School in a northern metropolitan borough. (Billsdyck is a pseudonym). Once again we are grateful to staff at the school for giving us access to their policy.

EDGEWICK COMMUNITY NURSERY AND PRIMARY SCHOOL EQUAL OPPORTUNITIES POLICY DOCUMENT

STATEMENT OF INTENT

In adopting and endorsing Coventry City Councils' equal opportunities policy document, we are committed at Edgewick Community Primary School to the provision of a learning environment for the local community in which each person involved in the processes of teaching and learning is accorded equality of esteem and value.

Principles

I *The School*

1.1 Our concern is for the whole child.

The staff will work to develop as fully as we can the intellectual, social, physical and aesthetic skills and aptitudes of each child at Edgewick, and to develop in each child a sense of self-esteem.

1.2 We are committed to enabling each child to have access to our whole school curriculum, of which the National Curriculum is a part.

1.3 We are committed to the eventual eradication of stereotypes and negative assumptions based on ethnicity, gender, social class and disability.

1.4 We are committed to a pro-active approach to issues of sexism, racism and discrimination against those who are differently abled, and will therefore vigorously pursue a policy of anti-sexist and anti-racist teaching and promote positive images and understandings of groups in society against whom there is widespread and institutionalized discrimination.

II *The Community*

2.1 We will be sensitive and responsive to the needs of our local community and promote the well-being of all its ethnic, religious and social groups.

2.2 We will provide, within the limitations of our buildings and budget, activities which the local community requires which accord with school and LEA policy.

2.3 In line with the LEA policy on adult education, we will ensure access to what we provide, so that we do not unknowingly exclude anyone on grounds of gender, ethnicity, disability or economic circumstance.

2.4 In line with LEA policy on adult education we will encourage the participation of adults in the planning, evaluation and resourcing of their own learning.

2.5 It is our aim that:
community staff
teaching staff
ancillary staff and
school governors
should provide a balanced representation of the sexes, ethnic and social groupings, so that we reflect the community in which we are situated, and provide children and adults with positive role models.

Approaches

I *The School*

1.1 We will promote each child's self-esteem.
 i) by valuing her/his contribution to the school in whatever area s/he achieves success, and by keeping ongoing records of achievement.
 ii) by our methods of evaluation, assessment and reporting to both the child and his/her parents.
 iii) by our behaviour and use of language.

1.2 We will enable each child to have access to the curriculum.
 i) by our selection of themes within the National Curriculum which are of perceived relevance to the background and experience of the children.

159

ii) by the selection of appropriate materials to facilitate (i) above.

iii) by ensuring that no area of the curriculum is seen as inappropriate for girls or boys to pursue.

iv) by the careful selection of materials and resources to facilitate (iii) above.

v) by the provision of materials and resources appropriate to those children who, at any time, are designated as having special educational needs.

1.3 We will progressively work for the eradication of stereotypes and negative assumptions about ethnic groups, women, working class pupils and those differently abled.

i) by monitoring all proposed new resources for bias (including omission).

ii) by evaluating current resources and improving on them, or using them critically.

iii) by monitoring school and classroom organization and practices, and by changing those practices which promote or legitimate stereotyping.

iv) by the use of examples of people who run counter to common stereotypes as an integral part of all our teaching.

v) by the use of people from outside agencies whose occupations run counter to common stereotypes.

vi) by the provision of bilingual support where necessary.

1.4 We will counter incidents of sexist, racist and discriminatory behaviour.

i) by providing good adult role models.

ii) by establishing norms of behaviour which declare any form of abuse to be unacceptable.

iii) by dealing with incidents as they arise and logging them.

iv) by integrating anti-racist and anti-sexist education into the routine teaching and organization of the school.

II *The Community*

1.1/1.2

We will respond to the needs of the local community.

i) by staff maintaining contact with other local community groups.

ii) by ongoing dialogue with the parents and other adults involved with children in school.

iii) by consultation with parent governors as representatives of the local community.

iv) by the provision of accessible multilingual information sheets, adverts, letters etc.

1.3 We will ensure access to what we provide.

i) by appropriate staffing, paying attention to the community's cultural needs.

ii) by establishing what are the appropriate times of day for different activities.

iii) by the provision of a suitable environment for women's activities.

iv) by the provision of creche facilities.

v) by a low-or no-charge policy.

vi) by appropriate arrangements for physical access to buildings for differently abled people.

1.4 We will ensure participation of adult learners.

i) by involving them in the planning of courses and in their content.

ii)   by asking participants to evaluate courses and acting on feedback.

iii) by making group decisions about the resourcing of classes.

1.5   We will ensure progression towards representative and balanced groups of staff and governors.

i)   by monitoring applicants according to gender and ethnicity.

ii)   by encouraging and enabling members of under-represented groups to apply for posts, or seek election to the governing body of the school.

iii) by appropriate advertisement and/or information about jobs/posts by the use of multilingual publicity and existing community networks.

iv)   by emphasizing the school's firm commitment to equal opportunities in all aspects of its life.

This policy document is intended to be provisional, and is therefore open to development and change. It will be supported by papers, workshop materials, check-lists etc. in order that we can continuously monitor, develop and improve our practice.

BILLSDYCK SECONDARY SCHOOL EQUAL OPPORTUNITIES POLICY

Equal Opportunities at Billsdyck School means that no member of the school community should be made to feel that their sex, race, religion, physical or personal characteristics place limitations on their personal development. We want all young people to have a positive view of themselves which will help them to achieve the highest possible standards in all areas of school life and in the future. It will also help them to develop a sense of mutual respect and co-operation.

We work towards this aim by creating a happy, productive atmosphere, being assertive in dealing with racial and sexual harassment and delivering a curriculum which is free from prejudice and stereotyping. We are actively conscious of the importance of positive imaging, praise and encouragement and of the need to constantly question our preconceptions and values. In order to support the realization of our aim, each curriculum area has access to a substantial equal opportunities resource library and is represented on the school's Equal Opportunities Working Party. This meets regularly to review aspects of the hidden and formal curriculum and to promote and encourage awareness of relevant issues. Currently, the group is working on an expansion of this policy in the form of a comprehensive and practical guide for staff.

A member of the Working Party is also a member of the TVEI(E)'s Cluster Equal Opportunities Working Party.

BIBLIOGRAPHY

Acker, S. (1983) Women and teaching. In S. Walker and L. Barton (eds), *Gender, Class and Education*. Lewes: Falmer.

Acker, S. (1986) What feminists want from education. In A. Hartnett and M. Naish (eds), *Education and Society Today*. Lewes: Falmer.

Acker, S. (1988) Teachers, gender and resistance. *British Journal of Sociology of Education*, **9**(3), 307–22.

Acker, S. (ed.) (1989) *Teachers, Gender and Careers*. Basingstoke: Falmer.

Adelman, C. (1979) Unpublished material on nursery education, cited by S. Delamont, *Sex Roles and the School*. London: Routledge (1990).

Aggleton, P. and Whitty, G. (1985) Rebels without a cause. *Sociology of Education*, **58**(1), 60–72.

Al-Khalifa, E. (1989) Management by halves: women teachers and school management. In H. De Lyon and F. Widdowson Migniuolo (eds), *Women Teachers: Issues and Experiences*. Milton Keynes: Open University Press.

Allen, I. (1987) *Education in Sex and Personal Relationships*. London: Policy Studies Institute.

Althusser, L. (1971) *Lenin and Philosophy*. London: New Left Books.

Anti-sexist Working Party (1985) 'Look Jane Look': anti-sexist initiatives in primary schools. In G. Weiner (ed.), *Just a Bunch of Girls*. Milton Keynes: Open University Press.

Antonouris, G. and Wilson, J. (1989) *Equal Opportunities in Schools; New Dimensions in Topic Work*. London: Cassell.

Anyon, J. (1983) Intersections of gender and class: accommodation and resistance by working class and affluent females to contradictory sex-role ideologies. In S. Walker and L. Barton (eds), *Gender, Class and Education*. Lewes: Falmer Press.

Arnot, M. (1983) A cloud over co-education: an analysis of the forms of transmission of class and gender relations. In S. Walker and L. Barton (eds), *Gender, Class and Education*. Lewes: Falmer Press.

Arnot, M. (1984) How shall we educate our sons? In R. Deem, (ed.), *Co-Education Reconsidered*. Milton Keynes: Open University Press.

Arnot, M. (1986) State education policy and girls' educational experiences. In V. Beechey and E. Whitelegg (eds), *Women in Britain Today*. Milton Keynes: Open University Press.

Arnot, M. (1989) Crisis or challenge: equal opportunities and the National Curriculum. NUT *Educational Review*, 3(2), 7–14.

Arnot, M. and Weiner, G. (eds) (1987) *Gender and the Politics of Schooling*. London: Hutchinson.

Asher, S.R. and Gottman, J.M. (1973) Sex of teacher and reading achievement. *Journal of Educational Psychology*, **65**.

Askew, S. and Ross, C. (1988) *Boys Don't Cry: Boys and Sexism in Education*. Milton Keynes: Open University Press.

Aspinwall, K. and Drummond, M.J. (1989) Socialised into primary teaching. In H. De Lyon and F. Widdowson Migniuolo (eds), *Women Teachers: Issues and Experiences*. Milton Keynes: Open University Press.

Assessment of Performance Unit (APU) (1982) *Mathematical Development, Primary Survey Report*, No. 3. London: HMSO.

Baker Miller, (1986) *Toward a New Psychology of Women*. Harmondsworth: Penguin.

Ball, S. (1981) *Beachside Comprehensive*. Cambridge: Cambridge University Press.

Ball, S. (1987) *The Micro-Politics of the School*. London: Methuen.

Ball, S. (1990) *Foucault in Schools*. London: Routledge.

Ball, S. and Goodson, I. (eds) (1984) *Teachers' Lives and Careers*. Lewes: Falmer.

Bandura, A. (ed.) (1971) *Psychological Modeling: Conflicting Theories*. Chicago: Aldine Atherton.

Barnes, D. (1976) *From Communication to Curriculum*. Harmondsworth: Penguin.

Barron, R. and Norris, G. (1976) Sexual division and the dual labour market. In D.L. Barker and S. Allen, *Dependence and Exploitation in Work and Marriage*. London: Longman.

Becker, H. (1963) *Outsiders: Studies in the Sociology of Deviance*. New York: Free Press.

Beechey, V. (1979) On patriarchy. *Feminist Review*, **3**, 66–82.

Benn, C. (1989) Preface to H. De Lyon and F. Widdowson Migniuolo (eds), *Women Teachers: Issues and Experiences*. Milton Keynes: Open University Press.

Bennett, J. and Forgan, R. (eds) (1991) *There's Something about a Catholic Girl*. London: Virago.

Berger, P. (1976) *Sociology: A Biographical Approach*. Harmondsworth: Penguin.

Birke, L. (1983) Nature and Culture, Units 2 and 3 of U221, *The Changing Experience of Women*. Milton Keynes: Open University Press.

Blom, G.E. (1971) Sex differences in reading ability. In S.G. Zimet, *Print and Prejudice*. London: Hodder & Stoughton.

Blyth, W.A.L. (1960) The sociometric study of children's groups in English schools. *British Journal of Education Studies*, **8**, 127–47.

Blyton, E. (1989) *The Secret Seven*. London: Hodder & Stoughton. (This was the thirty-first impression of the book.)

Board of Education (1926) *The Education of the Adolescent* (The Hadow Report). London: HMSO.

Bowles, S. and Gintis, H. (1976) *Schooling in Capitalist America*. London: Routledge & Kegan Paul.

Bradberry, J.S. (1989) Gender differences in mathematical attainment at 16+. *Educational Studies*, **15**(3), 301–14.

Braman, O. (1977) Comics. In J. King and M. Stott (eds), *Is This Your Life?* London: Virago.

Breakwell, G.M. and Weinberger, B. (1987) Young women in gender-atypical jobs. London: Department of Employment.

Brighton Women and Science Group (eds) (1980) *Alice through the Microscope: The Power of Science over Women's Lives*. London: Virago.

Brittain, V. (1933) *Testament of Youth*. London: Gollancz.

Browne, N. and France, P. (eds) (1986) *Untying the Apron Strings*. Milton Keynes: Open University Press.

Burchell, H. and Millman, V. (eds) (1989) *Changing Perspectives on Gender*. Milton Keynes: Open University Press.

Burgess, R. (1988) Points and posts: Teacher careers in a comprehensive school. In A. Green and S. Ball (eds), *Progress and Inequality in Comprehensive Education*. London: Routledge.

Burgess, H. (1989a) A sort of career: women in primary schools. In C. Skelton (1989) (ed.), *Whatever Happens to Little Women?* Milton Keynes: Open University Press.

Burgess, R. (1989b) Something you learn to live with? Gender and inequality in a comprehensive school. *Gender and education*, **1**(2), 155–65.

Burstall, S. (1914) In C. Chisholme, *The Medical Inspection of Girls in Secondary Schools*. London: Longmans.

Buswell, C. (1981) Sexism in school routines and classroom practice. *Durham and Newcastle Research Review*.

Byrne, E. (1978) *Women and Education*. London: Tavistock.

Cairns, J. and Inglis, B. (1989) A content analysis of ten popular history textbooks for primary schools with particular emphasis on the role of women. *Educational Review*, **41**(3), 221–6.

Calder, P. (forthcoming) Different discourses? Psychology and feminism at the interface: women, childcare and the training of childcare workers. *Gender and Education*.

Campbell, J.M. (1908) The effect of adolescence on the brain of the girl. Paper presented to the AUWT meeting, 23 May.

Carr, L. (1989) Equal opportunities – policy and legislation after ERA. *NUT Education Review*, **3**(2).

Carter, A. (1988) *The Politics of Women's Rights*. London: Longman.

Central Advisory Council for Education (CACE) (1959) *15–18* (The Crowther Report). London: HMSO.

Central Advisory Council for Education (1962) *Half Our Future* (The Newsom Report). London: HMSO.

Central Advisory Council for Education (1967) *Children and Their Primary Schools* (The Plowden Report). London: HMSO.

Chodorow, N. (1974) Family structure and feminine personality. In M. Rosaldo and L. Lamphere (eds), *Women, Culture and Society*. Stanford: Stanford University Press.

Chodorow, N. (1978) *The Reproduction of Mothering*. Los Angeles: University of California Press.

Clarricoates, K. (1980a) The importance of being Earnest, Emma, Tom, Jane. In R. Deem (ed.), *Schooling for Women's Work*. London: Routledge & Kegan Paul.

Clarricoates, K. (1980b) All in a day's work. In D. Spender and E. Sarah (eds), *Learning to Lose*. London: Women's Press.

Cockburn, C. (1987) *Two Track Training*. London: Macmillan.

Coleman, J.C. (1980) *The Nature of Adolescence*. London: Methuen.

Coles, B. and Maynard, M. (1990) Moving towards a fair start: equal gender opportunities and the careers service. *Gender and Education*, **2**(3), 297–309.

Connell, R.W. (1983) *Which Way Is Up? Essays on Class, Sex and Culture*. London: Allen & Unwin.

Connell, R.W. (1987) *Gender and Power*. London: Polity Press.

Connell, R.W. (1989) Cool guys, swots and wimps; the interplay of masculinity and education. *Oxford Review of Education*, **15**(3), 291–303.

Consultative Committee of the Board of Education (CCBE) (1926) *The Education of the Adolescent* (The Hadow Report). London: HMSO.

Cornbleet, A. and Libovitch, S. (1983) Anti-sexist initiatives in a mixed comprehensive school; a case study. In A. Wolpe and J. Donald (eds), *Is There Anyone Here from Education?* London: Pluto Press.

Corson, D. (forthcoming) Language, gender and education: a critical review linking social justice and power. *Gender and Education*.

Culley, L. (1986) *Gender Differences and Computing in Secondary Schools*. Loughborough: Loughborough University of Technology.

Cunnison, S. (1989) Gender joking in the staffroom. In S. Acker (ed.), *Teachers, Gender and Careers*. Basingstoke: Falmer.

Dale, R.R. (1969) *Mixed or Single Sex Schools*. See also Vol. II (1971) and Vol. III (1974). London: Routledge & Kegan Paul.

Dalla Costa, M. and James, S. (1972) *The Power of Women and the Subversion of the Community*. Bristol: The Falling Wall Press.

David, M.E. (1978) The family-education couple: towards an analysis of the William Tyndale dispute. In G. Littlejohn *et al.*, *Power and the State*. London: Croom Helm.

Davidoff, L. (1973) *The Best of Circles*. London: Croom Helm.

Davidson, H. (1985) Unfriendly myths about women teachers. In J. Whyte *et al.*, (eds), *Girl Friendly Schooling*. London: Routledge & Kegan Paul.

Davie, R. *et al.* (1972) *From Birth to Seven*. London: Longman.

Davies, B. (1982) *Life in the Classroom and Playground: The Accounts of Primary School Children*. London: Routledge & Kegan Paul.

Davies, B. (1989) *Frogs and Snails and Feminist Tales: Pre-school Children and Gender*. Sydney: Allen & Unwin.

Davies, L. (1984) *Pupil Power, Deviance and Gender in School*. Lewes: Falmer Press.

Davin, A. (1978) Imperialism and motherhood. *History Workshop Journal*, **5**, 9–15.

Deem, R. (1978) *Women and Schooling*. London: Routledge & Kegan Paul.

Deem, R. (1980) *Schooling for Women's Work*. London: Routledge & Kegan Paul.

Deem, R. (ed.) (1984) *Co-education Reconsidered*. Milton Keynes: Open University Press.

Delamont, S. (1976) The girls most likely to: cultural reproduction and the Scottish elites. *Scottish Journal of Sociology*, **1**(1), 29–43.

Delamont, S. (1978) The contradictions in ladies' education *and* The domestic ideology and women's education. In S. Delamont and L. Duffin (eds), *The Nineteenth Century Woman: Her Cultural and Physical World*. London: Croom Helm.

Delamont, S. (1980) *Sex Roles and the School*. London: Methuen.

Delamont, S. (1989) *Knowledgeable Women: Structuralism and the Reproduction of Elites*. London: Routledge.

Delamont, S. (1990) *Sex Roles and the School* (2nd Edition). London: Routledge.

De Lyon, H. (1989) Sexual harassment. In H. De Lyon and F. Widdowson Migniuolo (eds), *Women Teachers: Issues and Experiences*. Milton Keynes: Open University Press.

De Lyon, H. and Widdowson Migniuolo, F. (1989) Equality issues in school life. In H. De Lyon and F. Widdowson Migniuolo (eds), *Women Teachers: Issues and Experiences*. Milton Keynes: Open University Press.

DES (1975) *Curricular Differences for Boys and Girls: An Education Survey*. London: HMSO.

DES (1984) *Initial Teacher Training: Approval of Courses*. Circular No. 3/84, 13 April.

DES (1987) *DES Task Group on Assessment and Testing: A Report*. London: HMSO.

DES (1989) *From Policy to Practice*. London: HMSO.

DES (1989a) *Statistics of Education: Teachers in Service, 1986*. London: HMSO.

DES (1989b) *Survey of Secondary Staffing (England)*. London: HMSO.

DES (1989c) *Future Arrangements for the Accreditation of Courses of Initial Teacher Training: A Consultation Document*. Circular No. 3/84, 13 April.

DES (1989d) *Discipline in Schools*. London: HMSO.

DES (1991) *Science in the National Curriculum*. London: HMSO.

Douglas, J.W.B. (1964) *The Home and the School*. London: MacGibbon & Kee.

Dove, L. (1975) The hopes of immigrant school children. *New Society*, 10 April.

Draper, J. (1992) *The Creation of Lymescraft School: An Ethnographic Study of Some Aspects of a School Merger*. Unpublished Ph. D. thesis, Open University, Milton Keynes.

Dyhouse, C. (1977) Good wives and little mothers: social anxieties and the school girls' curriculum 1890–1920. *Oxford Review of Education*, 3(2).

Dyhouse, C. (1981) *Girls Growing up in Late Victorian and Edwardian England*. London: Routledge & Kegan Paul.

Ebutt, D. (1981) Science options in a girls' grammar school. In A. Kelly, *The Missing Half*. Manchester: Manchester University Press.

Eden, C. and Aubrey, K. (1988) YTS and gender: continuity or challenge. In B. Coles (ed), *Young Careers*. Milton Keynes: Open University Press.

Egan, B. (1990) Design and technology in the primary classroom: equalising opportunities. In E. Tutchell (ed), *Dolls and Dungarees*. Milton Keynes: Open University Press.

Elliot, J. (1974) Sex role constraints on freedom of discussion: a neglected reality of the classroom. *The New Era*, 55(6), 147–56.

Engels, F. (no date) *The Origin of the Family, Private Property and the State*. Moscow: Foreign Languages Publishing House. (First published 1884.)

EOC (1982) Report of conference on equal opportunities: what's in it for boys? Manchester: EOC.

EOC (1985) *Equal Opportunities and The Woman Teacher: Guidelines for the Elimination of Sex and Marriage Discrimination and the Promotion of Equality of Opportunity in Teacher Employment*. Manchester: EOC.

EOC (1987) The response of the EOC to the consultative document on the National Curriculum 5-16. Manchester: EOC.

EOC (1989) *Some Facts about women*. Manchester: EOC.

EOC (1990) *Some Facts about women*. Manchester: EOC.

EOC/London Borough of Croydon (1983) *Information Technology in Schools*. Manchester: EOC.

EOC/London Borough of Croydon (1985) *Girls and Information Technology*. Manchester: EOC.

ESRC (1988) *Girls and Mathematics: Some Lessons for the Classroom*. London: Economic and Social Research Council.

Evetts, J. (1989) The internal labour market for primary teachers. In S. Acker (ed.), *Teachers, Gender and Careers*. Lewes: Falmer.

Fagot, B.I. (1985) Beyond the reinforcement principle: another step toward understanding sex role development. *Developmental Psychology*, **26**(6), 129-35.

Fawcett Society (1987) *Starting Early: Equal Opportunities in the Primary School*. London: Fawcett Society.

Fawcett Society (1988) *Exams for the Boys; A Report into the Sex Bias in G.C.E Papers 1987*. London: Fawcett Society.

Fennena, E. (1983) Success in mathematics. In M. Marland (ed), *Sex Differentiation and Schooling*. London: Heinemann.

Fine, M. (1988) Sexuality, schooling and adolescent females: the missing discourse of desire. *Harvard Educational Review*, **5**(1), 29-53.

Firestone, S. (1979) *The Dialectic of Sex*. London: Cape.

Frazier, N. and Sadker, M. (1973) *Sexism in School and Society*. New York: Harper & Row.

French, J. (1990) *The Education of Girls*. London: Cassell.

Freud, S. (1977a) Some psychical consequences of the anatomical distinctions between the sexes. In *Standard Edition of the Complete Works of Sigmund Freud*, Vol. 19. London: Hogarth Press.

Freud, S. (1977b) Three essays on the theory of sexuality. In *Standard Edition of the Complete Works of Sigmund Freud*, Vol. 7. London: Hogarth Press.

Fuller, M. (1980) Black girls in a London comprehensive school. In R. Deem (ed), *Schooling for Women's Work*. London: Routledge & Kegan Paul.

Furlong, J. (1976) Interaction sets in the classroom. In M. Stubbs and S. Delamont (eds), *Readings on Interaction in the Classroom*. London: Furlong.

Galton, M. (1981) Differential treatment of boys and girls during science lessons. In A. Kelly (ed)., *The Missing Half*. Manchester: Manchester University Press.

Gilbert, R. (1984) *The Impotent Image: Reflections of Ideology in the Secondary School Curriculum*. Lewes: Falmer.

Gill, I. (1989) Trying not just to survive: a lesbian teacher in a boys' school. In L. Holly (ed.), *Girls and Sexuality*. Milton Keynes: Open University Press.

Gilligan, C. (1984) *In a Different Voice*. Cambridge, MA: Harvard University Press.

Goddard-Spear, M. (1989) Sex bias in science teachers' ratings of work. In contributions to the second GASAT conference, Oslo.

Goldberg, S. (1974) *The Inevitability of Patriarchy*. London: Temple Smith.

Graf, R.G. and Riddell, J. (1972) Sex differences in problem solving as a function of problem context. *Journal of Educational Research*, **65**(10), 451–2.

Grant, M. (1983) Craft, Design and Technology. In J. Whylde (ed.), *Sexism in the Secondary Curriculum*. London: Harper & Row.

Grant, R. (1987) Job hopes and career plans – heading for the top. Paper presented at conference, St Hilda's College, Oxford, September.

Grant, R. (1989) Women teachers' career pathways: towards an alternative model of career. In S. Acker (ed.), *Teachers, Gender and Careers*. Lewes: Falmer.

Gray, J. (1981) A biological basis for the sex differences in achievement in science? In A. Kelly (ed), *The Missing Half*. Manchester: Manchester University Press.

Greer, G. (1981) *The Female Eunuch*. London: Granada.

Griffith, C. (1985) *Typical Girls*. London: Routledge & Kegan Paul.

Hall, S. and Jefferson, T. (eds) (1976) *Resistance through Rituals*. London: Hutchinson.

Halson, J. (1989) The sexual harassment of young women. In L. Holly, *Girls and Sexuality: Teaching and Learning*. Milton Keynes: Open University Press.

Hansard Society Commission (1990) *Report on Women at the Top*. London: Hansard Society for Parliamentary Government.

Hanson, D. and Herrington, M. (1976) *From College to Classroom: The Probationary Year*. London: Routledge & Kegan Paul.

Hanson, J. (1987) *Equality Issues, Permeation and a PGCE Programme*. Unpublished M.Ed. dissertation, University of Sheffield.

Harding, J. (1979) Sex differences in examination performance at 16+. *Physics Education*, **14**, 280–91.

Harding, J. (1983) *Switched Off*. London: Longman.

Hargreaves, D. (1967) *Social Relations in a Secondary School*. London: Routledge & Kegan Paul.

Hart, R.A. (1979) *Children's Experience of Place: A Developmental Study*. New York: Irvington.

Hearn, G. (1987) *The Gender of Oppression*. Brighton: Harvester.

Hebdidge, D. (1975) The meaning of Mod. In S. Hall *et al.* (eds), *Resistance through Rituals*. London: Hutchinson.

Henry, J. (1963) *Culture against Man*. New York: Random House.

Herbert, C.M.H. (1989) *Talking of Silence: The Sexual Harassment of Schoolgirls*. Lewes: Falmer.

Hilsum, S. and Start, K.B. (1974) *Promotion and Careers in Teaching*. Slough: NFER.

Hinkley, S.M. (1987) *The TVEI Experience*. Sheffield: MSC.

HMI (1975) *Report on Curricular Differences in Schools*. London: HMSO.

HMI (1979) *Report on Aspects of Secondary Education*. London: HMSO.

HMI (1980) *Girls and Science: Matters for Discussion*. No. 13. London: HMSO.

Hodgeon, J. (1988) A Woman's World? A Report on a Project in Cleveland Nurseries on Sex Differentiation in the Early Years. Unpublished report sponsored jointly by Cleveland Education Committee and the EOC.

Holly, L. (1985) Mary, Jane and Virginia Woolf: ten-year-old girls talking. In G. Weiner, (ed.) *Just a Bunch of Girls*. Milton Keynes: Open University Press.

Holly, L. (1989) *Girls and Sexuality: Teaching and Learning*. Milton Keynes: Open University Press.

Horner, M. (1971) Femininity and success achievement – a basic inconsistency. In M.H. Garskov (ed.) *Roles Women Play*. CA: Brooks Cole.

Horney, K. (1926) The flight from motherhood. *International Journal of psychoanalysis*, **7**, 324–39.

Hughes, B., Smith, B., Agar, R. and Martin, J. (*et al.*) (1976) *The Woman Teacher: The Report of an Enquiry Conducted by a Group of Northamptonshire Deputy Heads and Senior Mistresses into the Attitudes of Women Teachers towards Their Teaching Careers*. Unpublished.

Hughes, M. (1934) *A London Child of the Seventies*. Oxford: Oxford University Press.

Hughes, M. (1936) *A London Girl of the Eighties*. Oxford: Oxford University Press.

Hughes, P. (1989) Four reasons why women don't become heads. Letter to *Times Educational Supplement*, 6 October.

Hunt, F. (1987) (ed.) *Lessons for Life: The Schooling of Girls and Women 1850–1950*. Oxford: Basil Blackwell.

Hutt, C. (1972) *Males and Females*. Harmondsworth: Penguin.

ILEA (1982) Sex Differences and Achievement. *Research and Statistical Report*, RS 823/82. London: ILEA.

ILEA (1987) *Primary Matters*. London: ILEA.

Ingelby, J.D. and Cooper, E. (1974) How teachers perceive first year school children. *Sociology*, **8**(3), 463–73.

Isaacson, Z. (1988) The marginalisation of girls in mathematics: some causes and some remedies. In D. Pimm (ed.), *Mathematics, Teachers and Children*. Sevenoaks: Hodder and Stoughton.

Joffe, L. and Foxman, D. (1984) Assessing mathematics: 5. Attitudes and sex differences. *Mathematics in School*, **13**(4), 95–107.

Jones, C. (1985) Sexual tyranny in mixed-sex schools: an in-depth study of male violence. In G. Weiner (ed.), *Just a Bunch of Girls*. Milton Keynes: Open University Press.

Jones, C. and Mahony, P. (eds) (1989) *Learning Our Lines: Sexuality and Social Control in Education*. London: Women's Press.

Jungman, A. (1986) *Lucy and the Big Bad Wolf*. London: Grafton Books.

Kagen, J. (1964) Acquisition and significance of sex typing and sex role identity. In J.L. Hoffman and X.X. Russell (eds), *Review of Child Development Research*. CA: Sage Foundation.

Kant, L. (1985) A question of judgment. In J. Whyte *et al.* (eds), *Girls Friendly Schooling*. London: Routledge & Kegan Paul.

Kant, L. (1987) National Curriculum: notionally equal. *NUT Education Review*, **1**(2), 41–4.

Kelly, A. (ed.) (1981) *The Missing Half*. Manchester: Manchester University Press.

Kelly, A., Whyte, J. and Smart, B. (1984) *Girls into Science and Technology: Final Report*. GIST, Department of Sociology, University of Manchester.

Kessler, S. and McKenna, W. (1985) *Gender: An Ethnomethodological Approach*. Chicago: University of Chicago Press.

King, R. (1978) *All Things Bright and Beautiful?* Chichester: Wiley.

Kohlberg, L. (1966) A cognitive-developmental analysis of children's sex-role concepts and attitudes. In E. Maccoby (ed.), *The Development of Sex Differences*. Stanford, CA: Stanford University Press.

Lacey, C. (1970) *Hightown Grammar*. Manchester: Manchester University Press.

La Fontaine, J.S. (1978) *Sex and Age as Principles of Social Differentiation*. London: Academic Press.

Lake, M. (1975) Are we born into our sex roles or programmed into them? *Women's Day*, January.

Lambart, A.M. (1976) The sisterhood. In M. Hammersley and P. Woods (eds), *The Process of Schooling*. London: Routledge & Kegan Paul.

Land, H. (1986) Women and children last: reform of social security. In M. Brenton and C. Ungerson (eds), *Yearbook of Social Policy 1985–1986*. London: Routledge & Kegan Paul.

Laquer, T. (1990) *Making Sex, Body and Gender: From the Greeks to Freud*, Cambridge, MA: Harvard University Press.

Lawlor, S. (1990) Speech at conference on teacher education, Centre for Policy Studies, December.

Lawlor, S. (1990) *Teachers Mistaught*. London: Centre for Policy Studies.

Lee, A. (1980) Together we learn to read and write: sexism and literacy.

In D. Spender and E. Sarah (eds), *Learning to Lose*. London: Women's Press.

Lees, S. (1983) How boys slag off girls. *New Society*, **13** October.

Lees, S. (1986) *Losing Out*. London: Hutchinson.

Lees, S. and Scott, M. (1990) Equal opportunities: rhetoric or action. *Gender and Education*, **2**(3), 333–44.

Lenskyj, H. (1990) Beyond plumbing and prevention. *Gender and Education*, **2**(2), 217–31.

Lister, M. (1984) *Princess Polly to the Rescue*. London: Methuen.

Llewellyn, M. (1980) Studying girls at school: the implications of confusion. In R. Deem (ed.), *Schooling for Women's Work*. London: Routledge & Kegan Paul.

Lloyd, B. and Archer, J. (1976) *Exploring Sex Differences*. London: Academic Press.

Lobban, G. (1975) Sex roles in reading schemes. *Education Review*, **27**(3), 202–10.

Lyons, G. (1981) *Teacher Careers and Career Perceptions*. Windsor: NFER-Nelson.

Mac an Ghaill, M. (1988) *Young, Gifted and Black*. Milton Keynes: Open University Press.

MacDonald, G. (1981) *Once a Week Is Ample, or the Intelligent Victorian's Guide to Sexuality and the Physical Passions: Quotations from Victorian Experts on Sex and Marriage*. London: Hutchinson.

McDonald, M. (1981) Schooling and the reproduction of class and gender relations. In R. Dale *et al.*, *Politics, Patriarchy and Practice*. Milton Keynes: Open University Press.

McDonald, M. (1983) Schooling and the reproduction of class and gender relations. In L. Barton *et al*, *Schooling, Ideology and the Curriculum*. Lewes: Falmer.

McFadden, M. (1984) Anatomy of difference: towards a classification of feminist theory. *Women's Studies International Forum*, 7(8), 495–504.

MacKinnon, C. (1983) Feminism, Marxism, method and the state. In E. Abel (ed.), *The Signs Reader*. Chicago: University of Chicago Press.

McRobbie, A. (1978a), *Jackie*: an ideology of adolescent femininity. CCCS Occasional Paper.

McRobbie, A. (1978b) Working class girls and the culture of femininity. In Women's Studies Group (CCCS University of Birmingham), *Women Take Issue: Aspects of Women's Subordination*. London: Hutchinson.

McRobbie, A. (1980) Settling accounts with subculture: a feminist critique. *Screen Education*, **34**.

McRobbie, A. and Garber, J. (1976) Girls and subcultures. In S. Hall *et al.*, *Resistance through Rituals*. London: Hutchinson.

McRobbie, A. and Nava, M. (eds) (1984) *Gender and Generation*. London: Macmillan.

Maccia, E.S., Coleman, M.A. and Estep, M. (1975) *Women and Education*. Illinois, Thomas Springfield.

Maccoby, E.E. and Jacklin, C.N. (1974) *The Psychology of Sex Differences*. Stanford, CA: Stanford University Press.

Mahony, P. (1985) *Schools for the Boys*. London: Hutchinson.

Marks, P. (1976) Femininity in the classroom: an account of changing attitudes. In J. Mitchell and A. Oakley (eds), *The Rights and Wrongs of Women*. Harmondsworth: Penguin.

Marland, M. (1983) *Sex Differentiation in Schooling*. London: Heinemann.

Marsh, L. (1990) *Gender and Education: An Introduction to the Problem*. Scottish Consultative Council on the Curriculum.

Marsland, D. (1983) Youth. In A. Hartnett (ed.), *The Social Sciences in Educational Studies*. London: Heinemann.

Mason, N. and Jewson, D. (1986) The theory and practice of equal opportunities policies: liberal and radical approaches. *Sociological Review*, **34**(2), 307–34.

Mead, M. (1950) *Male and Female*. Harmondsworth: Penguin.

Measor, L. (1984) Gender and the sciences: Pupils' gender-based conceptions of school subjects. In M. Hammersley and A. Hargreaves (eds), *Curriculum Practice*. Lewes: Falmer.

Measor, L. (1989) Are you coming to see some dirty films today? Sex education and adolescent sexuality. In L. Holly (ed.), *Girls and Sexuality*. Milton Keynes: Open University Press.

Measor, L. and Woods, P. (1984) *Changing Schools*. Milton Keynes: Open University Press.

Meighan, R. (1986) (ed.) *A Sociology of Educating*. London: Cassell.

Menter, I. (1989) Teaching practice stasis: racism, sexism and school experience in initial teacher education. *British Journal of Sociology of Education*, **10**(4), 459–73.

Meyenn, R. (1980) School girl peer groups. In P. Woods (ed.), *Pupil Strategies*. London: Croom Helm.

Millett, K. (1971) *Sexual Politics*. London: Rupert Hart-Davis.

Millman, V. and Weiner, G. (1985) *Sex Differentiation in Schooling: Is There Really a Problem?* London: Longmans/Schools' Council.

Ministry of Education (1959) *15–18: Report of the Central Advisory Council for Education – England* (The Crowther Report). London: HMSO.

Mischel, W. (1966) A social learning view of sex differences in behaviour. In E.E. Maccoby (ed.), *The Development of Sex Differences*. Stanford, CA: Stanford University Press.

Mitchell, J. (1974) *Psychoanalysis and Feminism*. Harmondsworth: Penguin.

Morgan, C., Hall, V. and McKay, H. (1983) *The Selection of Secondary*

School Headteachers. Milton Keynes: Open University Press.

Moss, H. (1970) Sex, age and state as determinants of mother-infant interaction. In K. Danzinger (ed.), *Readings in Child Socialisation*. Oxford: Pergamon.

MSC (1984) *TVEI Review*. Sheffield: MSC.

Mungham, G. and Pearson, G. (1976) *Working Class Youth Cultures*. London: Routledge & Kegan Paul.

Murdock, G. and Phelps, G. (1973) *Mass Media and the Secondary School*. London: Macmillan (Schools' Council Publications).

Murphy, P. (1989) Assessment and gender. *NUT Educational Review*, 3(2).

Murphy, P. and Gott, R. (1984) *Science assessment Framework Age 13–15. Science Report for Teachers No. 2*. Association for Science Education.

Murphy, P. and Johnson, S. (1986) *Girls and Physics. Reflections on APU Survey Findings*. London: HMSO.

Murphy, P. and Moon, R. (eds) (1990) *Developments in Learning and Assessment*. Milton Keynes: Open University Press.

Murphy, R.J. (1981) Sex differences in objective test performance. *British Journal of Educational Psychology*, **52**.

Myers, K. (1987) *Genderwatch: Self Assessment Schedules for Use in Schools*. London: SCDC & EOC.

Neale, D.C., Gill, N. and Tismer, W. (1970) Relationship between attitudes to school subjects and school achievement. *Journal of Educational Psychology*, **63**.

Newsom, J. (1948) *The Education of Girls*. London: Faber & Faber.

Newson, J. and Newson, E. (1976) *Seven Years Old in the Home Environment*. London: Allen & Unwin.

NFER (1989) *Equal Opportunities for Girls and Boys within TVEI*. Sheffield: The Training Agency.

Nightingale, C. (1974) Sex roles in children's literature. In S. Allen, L. Sanders and J. Wallis (eds), *Conditions of Illusion*. Leeds: Feminist Press.

Nilan, P. (1991) Exclusion, inclusion and moral ordering in two girls' friendship groups. *Gender and Education*, 3(2).

Nilson, A.P. (1973) Women in children's literature. In E.S. Maccia *et al.* (eds), *Women and Education*. IL: Charles C Thomas.

Northam, J. (1982) Girls and boys in primary maths. *Books in Education*.

NUT (1988) *Towards Equality for Girls and Boys*. London: NUT.

NUT (1989) *The Educational Review*, 3(2).

NUT/EOC (1980) *Promotion and the Woman Teacher*. London: NUT/EOC.

Oakley, A. (1972) *Sex, Gender and Society*. London: Temple Smith.

O'Donnell, C.O. and Hall, P. (1988) *Getting Equal*. Sydney, Australia: Allen & Unwin.

O'Donovan, K.O. (1988) *Equality and Sex Discrimination Law*. Oxford: Basil Blackwell.

Open University (1981) Popular culture, class and schooling. Unit 9 for course E353 (*Society, Education and the State*). Milton Keynes: Open University Press.

Ord, F. and Quigley, J. (1985) Anti-sexism as good educational practice: what feminists can realistically achieve. In G. Weiner (ed.), *Just a Bunch of Girls*. Milton Keynes, Open University Press.

Orr, P. (1985) Sex bias in schools: national perspectives. In J. Whyte *et al.*, *Girl-Friendly Schooling*. Methuen: London.

Parker, H. (1976) *The View from the Boys*. Newton Abbot: David and Charles.

Partington, G. (1976) *Women Teachers in England and Wales*. Windsor: NFER–Nelson.

Payne, I. (1980) A working class girl in a grammar school. In D. Spender and E. Sarah (eds), *Learning to Lose*. London: Women's Press.

Peacock, S. and Shinkins, S. (1983) *Insight: A Review of the Insight Programme to Encourage More Girls to Become Professional Engineers*. Engineering Industry Training Board.

Pollard, A. (1985) *The Social World of the Primary School*. London: Cassell.

Poulantzas, N. (1969) The problems of the capitalist state. *New Left Review*, **58**, 67–79.

Prendergast, S. and Prout, A. (1987) Smile at him when you ask for the books. In T. Booth and D. Coulby (eds), *Producing and Reducing Disaffection*. Milton Keynes: Open University Press.

Purvis, J. (1981a) Women's life is essentially domestic; public life being confined to men. *History of Education*.

Purvis, J. (1981b) The double burden of class and gender in the schooling of working class girls in nineteenth century England, 1800–1870. In L. Barton and S. Walker (eds), *Schools, Teachers and Teaching*. Lewes: Falmer.

Purvis, J. (1991) *A History of Women's Education in England*. Milton Keynes: Open University Press.

Purvis, J. and Hales, M. (eds) (1983) *Achievement and Inequality in Education*. London: Routledge & Kegan Paul.

Reay, D. (1990) Working with boys. *Gender and Education*, **2**(3).

Reid, I. and Stratta, E. (eds) (1989) *Sex Differences in Britain*. Aldershot: Gower.

Robins, D. and Cohen, P. (1978) *Knuckle Sandwich: Growing up in the Working Class City*. Harmondsworth: Penguin.

Rosenthal, R. and Jacobson, L. (1968) *Pygmalion in the Classroom*. Eastbourne: Holt, Rinehart and Winston.

Rowbotham, S. (1975) *Hidden from History*. London: Pluto Press.

Rowbotham, S. (1979) The trouble with patriarchy. *New Statesman*, vol. **98**.

Rumbold, A. (1990) Speech given at International Conference on Equal Advances in Educational Management, Vienna.

Sadker, M. and Sadker, D. (1982) *Sex Equity Handbook for Schools*. London: Longman.

St John, C. (1932) The maladjustment of boys in certain elementary grades. *Educational Administration and Supervision*, **18**.

Saraga, E. and Griffiths, D. (1981) Biological inevitabilities or political choices? The future for girls in science. In A. Kelly (ed.), *The Missing Half*.

Sayers, J. (1987) Psychology and gender divisions. In G. Weiner and M. Arnot (eds), *Gender under Scrutiny: New Inquiries in Education*. London: Hutchinson.

Sedley, A. and Benn, M. (1982) *Sexual Harassment at Work*. London: National Council for Civil Liberties, Rights for Women Unit.

Serbin, L.A. (1978) Teachers, peers and play preferences. In B. Sprung (ed.), *Perspectives on Non-Sexist Early Childhood Education*. New York: Teachers' College Press.

Shakeshaft, C. (1986) A gender at risk. *Phi Delta Kappa*, March.

Sharpe, S. (1976) *Just Like a Girl*. Harmondsworth: Penguin.

Shaw, J. (1980) Education and the individual: schooling for girls, or mixed schooling – a mixed blessing. In R. Deem (ed.), *Schooling for Women's Work*.

Sheffield LAPP Team (1990) Case study: equal opportunities and the Sheffield curriculum initiative (LAPP). In H. Burchell and V. Millman, *Changing Perspectives on Gender*. Milton Keynes: Open University Press.

Short, G. and Carrington, B. (1989) Discourse on gender: the perceptions of children aged between six and eleven. In C. Skelton (ed.), *Whatever Happens to Little Women?* Milton Keynes: Open University Press.

Sikes, P. (1986) The Mid-Career Teacher: Adaptations and Motivation in a Contracting Secondary School System. Unpublished PhD thesis, University of Leeds.

Sikes, P. (1991) 'Nature took its course'. Student teachers and gender awareness. *Gender and Education*, **3**(2), 145–63.

Sikes, P., Measor, L. and Woods, P. (1985) *Teacher Careers: Crises and Continuities*. Lewes: Falmer.

Skeggs, B. (1986) Young Women and Further Education: A Case Study of Young Women's Experience of Caring Courses in a Local College. Unpublished PhD. thesis, University of Keele.

Skeggs, B. (1989) Gender differences in education. In I. Reid and E. Stratta (eds), *Sex Differences in Britain*. Aldershot: Gower.

Skelton, C. (1985) Gender Issues in a Primary Teacher Training Programme. Unpublished MA, University of York.

Skelton, C. (1987) A study of gender discrimination in a primary programme of teacher training. *Journal of education for teaching*, **13**(2), 163–75.

Skelton, C. (1989) And so the wheel turns . . . gender and initial teacher education. In C. Skelton (ed.), *Whatever Happens to Little Women?* Milton Keynes: Open University Press.

Skelton, C. and Hanson, J. (1989) Schooling the teachers: gender and ITE. In S. Acker (ed.), *Teachers, Gender and Careers*. Lewes: Falmer.

Skinner, R. and Cleese, J. (1982) *Families and How to Survive Them*. London: Methuen.

Smith, J. and Bells, S. (1989) *Women Secondary School Teachers in Warwickshire*. Warwickshire County Council.

Smith, L.S. (1978) Sexist assumptions and female delinquency. In C. Smart and B. Smart (eds), *Women, Sexuality and Social Control*. London: Routledge & Kegan Paul.

Smith, S. (1986) *Separate Tables!* London: HMSO.

Smith, S. (1987) *Separate Beginnings!* London: HMSO.

Smithers, A. and Hills, S. (1989) Recruitment to mathematics and physics teaching. *Research Papers in Education*, **4**(1), 3–21.

Spencer, H. (1867) *The Principles of Biology 2*. London (no publisher).

Spencer, M. (1976) Learning to read and the reading process. In *Language and Literacy*. London: Institute of Education.

Spender, D. (1979) *Man Made Language*. London: Routledge & Kegan Paul.

Spender, D. (1982) *Invisible Women: The Schooling Standard*. London: Readers and Writers Co-operative.

Spender, D. and Sarah, E. (eds) (1980) *Learning to Lose*. London: Women's Press.

Spender, D. and Sarah, E. (1982) *An Investigation of the Implications of Courses on Sex Discrimination in Teacher Education*. London: EOC.

Squirrell, G. (1989) In passing . . . teachers and sexual orientation. In S. Acker (ed.), *Teachers, Gender and Careers*. Lewes: Falmer.

Stacey, J. *et al.* (eds) (1974) *And Jill Came Tumbling After*. New York: Dell.

Stanworth, M. (1981) *Gender and Schooling: A Study of Sexual Divisions in the Classroom*. Pamphlet (7). London: WRRC.

Stanworth, M. (1983) *Gender and Schooling*. London: Hutchinson.

Steedman, C. *The Times*, 5 November 1929; Underclass of women teachers revealed. *Times Educational Supplement*, 12 October 1990.

Steedman, C. (1982), *The Tidy House: Little Girls Writing*. London: Virago.

Stein, A.H. and Smithells, J. (1969) Age and sex differences in children's sex role standards about achievement. *Developmental Psychology*, **I**.

Stobart, G., Elwood, J. and Quinlon, M. (forthcoming) Gender bias in examinations: How equal are the opportunities?

Sturge, H.W. (1932) Foreword to M.G. Shaw, *Redland High School*.

Sutherland, M.B. (1981) *Sex Bias in Education*. Oxford: Blackwell.

Sutherland, M.B. (1983) Anxiety, aspirations and the curriculum. In M. Marland (ed.), *Sex Differentiation and Schooling*. London: Heinemann.

Sylva, K., Roy, C. and Painter, M. (1980) *Childwatching at Playgroup and Nursery School*. Grant McIntyre.

Swetman, R. (1989) Teaching sex education. The experiences of four teachers. In L. Holly (ed.), *Girls and Sexuality*. Milton Keynes: Open University Press.

Taylor, H. (1985) INSET for equal opportunities in the London Borough of Brent. In J. Whyte *et al.*, *Girl-Friendly Schooling*. Methuen: London.

Thompson, B. (1989) Teacher attitudes: complacency and conflict. In C. Skelton (ed.), *Whatever Happens to Little Women?* Milton Keynes: Open University Press.

Tong, R. (1988) *Feminist Thought: A Comprehensive Introduction*. London: Unwin Hyman.

Troyna, B. and Hatcher, R. (1992) *Racism in Children's Lives*. London: Routledge.

Tutchell, E. (ed.) (1990) *Dolls and Dungarees*. Milton Keynes: Open University Press.

Verrall, R. (1979) *Spearhead*, March.

Walby, S. (1985) *Patriarchy at Work*. Cambridge: Polity Press.

Walden, R. and Walkerdine, V. (1982) *Girls and Mathematics: The Early Years*. Bedford Way Paper 8. London: Institute of Education.

Walden, V. and Walkerdine, V. (1985) *Girls and Mathematics: From Primary to Secondary Schooling*. Bedford Way Paper 24. London: Institute of Education.

Walkerdine, V. (1981) Sex, power and pedagogy. *Screen Education*, **38**, 14–24.

Walkerdine, V. (1984) Developmental psychology and the child-centred pedagogy: the insertion of Piaget into early education. In Henriques *et al.*, *Changing the Subject*. London: Methuen.

Walters, A. (1978) Women writers and prescribed texts. Waste Papers. Presented at the National Association for the Teaching of English, Annual Conference, York.

Webb, M. (1989) Sex and gender in the labour market. In I. Reid and E. Stratta, *Sex Differences in Britain*. Aldershot: Gower.

Weightman, J. (1989) *Educational Management and Administration*, **17**(3).

Weiner, G. (1980) Sex differences in mathematical performance: a review of the research and possible action. In R. Deem, *Schooling for Women's Work*. London: Routledge & Kegan Paul.

Weiner, G. (ed.) (1985) *Just a Bunch of Girls*. Milton Keynes: Open University Press.

Weiner, G. (ed.) (1990) *The Primary School and Equal Opportunities*. London: Cassell.

Whitbread, A. (1988) Female teachers are women first; sexual harassment at work. In D. Spender and E. Sarah (eds), *Learning to Lose*. London: Women's Press.

Whyte, J. (1983a) *Beyond the Wendy House*. London: Longman.

Whyte, J. (1983b) Courses for teachers on sex differences and sex typing. *Journal of Education for Teaching*, 9(3), 235–48.

Whyte, J. (1985) *Girl Friendly Schooling*. London: Methuen.

Willis, E. (1975) The conservatism of *Ms*. In Redstockings (eds), *Feminist Revolution*. New York: Random House.

Willis, P. (1977) *Learning to Labour*. Farnborough: Saxon House.

Willms, J.D. and Kerr, P. (1987) Changes in sex differences in Scottish examination results. *Journal of Early Adolescence*, June.

Wilson, E. (1977) *Women and the Welfare State*. London: Tavistock.

Windass, A. (1989) Classroom practices and organisation. In C. Skelton (ed.), *Whatever Happens to Little Women?* Milton Keynes: Open University Press.

WISE (1984) The scheme has not been fully researched; for an account of it, see S. Delamont (1990) *Sex Roles and the School*.

Wolpe, A. (1989) *Within School Walls*. London: Routledge.

Woman Teacher (1939) Report of Speech at NAS Annual Conference, 21 April 1939.

Wood, J. (1984) Boys' sex talk: groping toward sexism? In A. McRobbie and M. Nava (eds), *Gender and Generation*. London: Hutchinson.

Woods, P. (1979) *The Divided School*. London: Routledge & Kegan Paul.

Zimmerman, D. and West, C. (1975) Sex roles, interruptions and silences in conversation. In B. Thorne and N. Henley (eds), *Language and Sex: Difference and Dominance*. Rowley, Newbury House, USA.

NAME INDEX

Subject Index

academic success, fear of
102–4
achievement, in secondary
schools 70–1
see also underachievement
adolescence 31–2, 91
deviance in 96–106
friendship groups in 92–5
and gender socialization
71–2
anti-sexist approach to equal
opportunities 125–6
appearance
and girls' friendship groups
93–4
teachers' comments on 65
art work 135, 136
assemblies, and equal
opportunities policies
128
assessment, in-school 77,
79, 140

behaviour
of boys towards girls in
school 29–30
social codes of 66–7, 83
of teachers and pupils in
classroom 80–1
biological determinism
theories of gender
differences 6–8
black feminists 21
black pupils 2
boys
and academically
successful women 103–4
behaviour towards girls in
school 29–30
conformist and deviant
103, 105
and deviance 96, 97, 103,
105

and equal opportunities
work 143
examination results 74,
139
and friendship groups 92–3
pre-school years 51–2
in primary schools 52–68
and psychoanalytic
theories 11–12, 31
sexual harassment by 85–6
teachers' expectations of
62–4, 79–80
and TVEI 130
working-class 2

careers
career patterns of teachers
67, 109–10
Crowther Report on 43–4
nineteenth-century
attitudes to 39–40
service in schools 86, 141
Catholics, and education for
girls 37, 40
child-rearing practices
and gender differences
11–12
and psychoanalytic
feminism 31
children's story books 134–5
chromosomes 6
class, *see* social class
classroom organization/
management
in primary schools 54–5
in secondary schools 81–2
clothing, *see* dress
co-education 44, 144
cognitive development
theories of gender
differences 10, 52
comprehensive schools 44
convents, education in 37

CPVE (Certificate of Pre-
Vocational Education)
45
Crowther Report (1959) 43–4
curriculum
access to, and equal
opportunities 132–3
anti-sexist approach
to 125–6
in convent schools 37
core 47, 76
and equal opportunities
policies 128–36
in nineteenth-century
middle-class girls'
schools 38
in primary schools 55–62
in state elementary
schools 41
and subject choice 72–7
see also hidden
curriculum; National
Curriculum; subject
choices

developmental theories of
girls' attitudes to school
99–100, 101
deviance 96–9
explanations for 99–106
display work, equal
opportunity themes 135
division of labour 23–4, 25,
26
domestic labour, Marxist
view of 23–4
drama 135, 136
dress
pre-school children 51
school uniform 54, 101
education
and liberal feminism 21
and psychoanalytic
feminism 31–2

182